WingChun

The Way of the Warrior

Fundamentals and Beyond of a Superior Martial Art

by Sifu K. Brand

International Academy of WingChun
14197 Berlin, Germany

ISBN
978-3-9825592-5-4

This book is a must-read for anyone who wants to achieve their full potential through the art of fighting. The journey towards this goal is paved with knowledge, discipline, and unwavering commitment to routines. Success is within reach for those who discover their unique path and possess the determination to master it.

About the Author

At the age of five, I began training in martial arts. In my case it was judo as my father was a judo trainer. As a teenager, other martial arts caught my interest and I started to experiment. Many years later, at the beginning of my military service, I discovered WingChun*. This art awakened far more than just an interest for me. Rather, it was a feeling as if I had been waiting for this art and it had arrived. Almost at the same time, I began training in Escrima, the art of weapons fighting.

My military career started after basic training in an air deployment group. After the first career training, I was deployed as the commander of a reconnaissance tank used by the NBC defence force. After my second career training, a few promotions and moves later, I followed the training to become a commando leader at the Army Combat Troops School. Accompanied by the lone fighter training coveted by the German Armed Forces and the corresponding award.

Multiple training such as object protection, evacuation measures, nuclear, biological and chemical defence were supplemented. After further mission-related training, including as a teacher at an army school, I was then deployed to the Army School for NBC Defence and Self-Protection to teach firefighting, disaster protection, rescue and recovery from rubble as well as abseiling from buildings in theory and practice.

Upon completion of over ten years of service with weapons, I left the military (in the 90s) to make my hobby, WingChun* my profession. Ten years later, after having opened training centres in eight countries, I founded the International Academy of WingChun. Led it as Grandmaster and after another ten years, the development of S.A.T, the martial art of a new era, was completed. Decade after decade, my path became clearer and clearer. Since childhood, I have dedicated myself to martial and military training. It was not enough for me to know only partial aspects about it, and so I found my way.

詠春

Table of Contents

I. Introduction

Martial arts can add far more to your life than the skills you acquire within it. I will: report to you on my research into the history of WingChun*, deal with general and scientific aspects, impart technical knowledge, share my experiences with you, and include spiritual perspectives.

I wrote this book not only for friends of martial arts but also for people who have recognized that there is always something to overcome in life and that the principles of martial arts are also the basis for success which can be extremely useful in other areas.

When I write WingChun, I mean my system, which I completely reformed during the 1990s. After completing my studies and research, I realised how much this brilliant system had been adapted to the spirit of the times. My only options were to get involved or start all over again.

When I write WingChun*, this is the name for all systems that developed from the original art. There are many spellings, so I want to be fair and include mine when I write WingChun*. How one writes this style in Latin script, from what one hears or understands from the sounds of the spoken Chinese characters 詠春, can be very different. Therefore, there are actually no right or wrong spellings. If one insisted on the only correct spelling, there would be no other option but to write 詠春. But even in this form, you can use your own, very personal calligraphy, which I expressed on the book's first pages. Many Grandmasters of the different styles of WingChun* each defined their systems with a personal spelling or with the addition of their name, which is also a good method of differentiation. Today, one can clearly recognize or easily identify which Grandmaster an instructor feels connected to by means of Western spelling or personal calligraphy.

Today there are some good systems taught which are well copied, but unfortunately, many misinterpreted systems exist that are badly copied. Finding one's way around these styles is almost impossible for the layperson. I can now look back on more than 50 years of martial arts experience, from when I started with WingChun* during the 80s. I know how to distinguish between the basic styles and how certain perspectives found their way into educational institutions around the world because I was involved and witnessed it.

Each of us can correct mistakes at any time and learn from them. Ignoring mistakes, especially when you recognize them yourself, just because it's more comfortable to keep doing what you've always done, I personally don't think is the attitude a martial artist should have. Those who are able to differentiate and, if necessary, also let go of the past can find their way or regain it.

About 45 years ago, the first schools of WingChun* existed in Europe. However, this "new art of self-defence" had its difficulties in surviving against the martial arts that had been established many years previously. Perhaps precisely because of the contrast to well-known concepts, a scientific method of defence that does not base itself on youthfulness and athleticism, but solely on the natural function of the human body and that leaves nothing to chance was completely unknown until that time. The drastic difference between an effective martial art that was created for war and the martial art that was developed for sporting competition was only known to a few at the time. Unfortunately, this misunderstanding remains widespread and has only improved marginally to date.

To this day, the opinion persists that you have to be big, strong and a top athlete in order to practice or master a martial art. We are so influenced by exaggerated representations that we believe what is suggested to us by the media after inadequate research. The manipulation even goes so far that men and women consider themselves sick if they do not conform to the "norm" set by a certain group of people. This negative attitude manifests itself in striking ways, causing people to gradually lose the ability to think objectively. The search and the desire for the dream state, dream body, dream weight, dream house, dream partner, dream job and dream vacation etc. make reality fade more and more into a distant memory.

The distinction between advertising campaigns, films and reality is becoming increasingly difficult in our remote-controlled society. We should finally wake up and accept the fact that we are who we are: big or small, strong or graceful, male or female etc. Some of these facts we cannot change and some we do not have to change because that is our individual Identity. Each of us is unique. Not only is the handsome, tall and well-trained man the “super martial artist". The reality of life teaches us otherwise.

It is hard to put into numbers how many incredibly capable women I have met throughout my martial arts career. These women stood out for their perseverance, will, and initially for their self-confidence. The powerful movements and technical ability of these women really exemplified their skills. I mention women here to make it clear that the scene does not only belong to men. Precisely because there are anatomical advantages for men, women should be treated with the appropriate respect. Once the level of an advanced student is reached, there are no discernible differences between the sexes in a technical sense. From this stage, only the technical level allows a distinction.

It took many years to establish WingChun* in the martial arts scene. One of the reasons for its slow rise was that there are no WingChun* tournaments held. This is an art of war developed for emergency situations, which would be misused by setting up rules to govern it. It must be mentioned at this point that WingChun* is not only an extremely effective form of self-defence, but also positively changes one's mental state of self-confidence, body and mind in a healthy and natural way, and vastly improves body coordination. Around 2000 years ago, during the Han Dynasty (206 BC to 220 AD), certain movement sequences and forms of various martial arts were used for therapeutic purposes in China. The greatest war heroes developed forms of movement, which were then translated as "inner work" to strengthen the body and maintain health.

But let's stick to self-defence. In a real defensive situation, there can be neither fixed attacks nor sporting techniques, everything must be allowed. Survival is the only thing at stake in such a situation, which means that in order to avoid any further risk, one must end the conflict as quickly as possible. WingChun* was designed to end a defensive situation within a few seconds. Not the notion of fighting, but the necessity of a quick victory, is the top priority. Actually, fighting has nothing to do with whether you win or not. In fact, anyone can fight. When I was young, I was amazed that there were so many fighters in martial arts but so few winners in tournaments. Even to those who had just lost a sporting fight, people said: "But you fought well." Moreover, in the end, everyone had fought.

The decisive factor is the victory, not the fight or how well you fought. The battle for victory doesn't have to look pretty.

It's all about winning and possibly suffering only minor injuries or none at all.

Why do you have to compete with others? Is a measurement even possible? In my opinion, in terms of martial arts, this is an illusion. If two fighters really want to compete, there should be neither spectators nor referees and, of course, no time limit and certainly no regulations. In addition, one should not separate according to weight classes or gender and the physical condition should play just as little a role as age and the technical (physical) possibilities that everyone exhibits. Such a fight would look starkly different then. Under these circumstances, which people would want to fight voluntarily if there was a risk of not surviving the fight or that very day?

In martial arts lessons, we don't fight against each other, but practice for the case of defence, in which we don't want to fight, but win unconditionally. A perfectly designed training program navigates the students through a fascinating art of movement in which all newly learned techniques and combinations can be applied immediately, even if they are not perfectly mastered. Nevertheless, studying martial arts cannot be compared to a course that you can complete quickly. Rather, one remains a constant student, always a seeker, moving forward to open up new realms.

The way is (already) the goal, and ultimately just the way we chose to go. The abundance of knowledge that this path offers us is the only thing that really has any value in this life. It is through mistakes that we can truly learn and grow, gain new insights that shape our character and expand our intellect. Anyone can learn, regardless of age. The past made us what we are today. The future is fiction that only gives us an abstract picture of the path ahead. We all build our future through our thoughts and the resulting actions at this very moment. As of today, you build tomorrow. So, think about what you have done or learnt today, because tomorrow it will be in your past, the one that shapes you. Each individual is responsible for their happiness. Welcome to the uniqueness of every moment.

After the urgently needed reform of WingChun*, I founded the "International Academy of WingChun". We toured the US, UK, Malaysia, France, Romania, the Philippines, Namibia and Germany. It has always been my wish to produce professional trainers, enthusiasts, who are constantly educating themselves, learning with love, and passing on their knowledge.

Learning a real martial art means constant physical and mental effort. A martial artist is a disciplined and proud individual who never stands still and continually improves in all areas of being.

II. The Choice Is Yours

a. Readiness for Self-Protection

The topic of self-defence as well as that of self-protection becomes more fascinating from year to year. We live in a world of constant change in a fast-paced society. Starting with the global political conflicts and domestic political confusion, which regularly makes us aware of our powerlessness. We experience changes in the areas of state leadership, upbringing, education, jobs, technology, food, attitudes to life, fashion, etc. This means that the feeling of permanence and stability falls by the wayside. Many lack a clear line in the almost unreasonable confusion of the constantly new standards. In the end, all of this often robs you of the perspectives and motivation for a carefree life.

The steady increase in violence is hard to miss and is ironically broadcast in the daily news along with its causes. Not a day goes by when we don't hear about various acts of violence in our immediate vicinity. Starting with violence in schools, drug-related crime of all kinds, sexual assault and so on. Unfortunately, these issues are still being treated like illnesses. Only the cause of this "disease" seems to remain a mystery. As long as you are not affected yourself, you do not want to deal with the topic of "violence". However, this diminishes the willingness to help oneself and especially others in emergency situations because education in this area is virtually non-existent.

The willingness and likelihood of aggressors to use violence is constantly increasing. At this point, I cannot comment on whether political or social inadequacies should be held responsible for this, but what is certain is that the way people deal with each other is turning into superficiality and reserved acceptance. The ego has run away from empathy. In a selfish society, rational thinking only protects one's own existence. The hope remains that love and compassion will not die out completely. Unfortunately, virtues such as modesty and honesty are often ridiculed. All this at a time when we focus on education and development.

Remember reports of various catastrophes in different countries around the world. Also remember that all of a sudden people became looters, thieves and murderers. As if all education, experience and hundreds of years of evolution are erased within a few hours and people from a technical and intellectual peak of development unexpectedly mutate into primates. The pillars of civilisation are highly unstable. The question often arises as to whether mankind was civilized or simply domesticated. What is going on in the minds of those affected, and how do their victims feel? These are the questions that have occupied me for years of silent observation. The dangers are present; we cannot ignore them. We are not safe anywhere, and that is a sad but real fact. Repression and ignorance prevent the development of knowledge, skill, and all that remains is hope.

A quarter of a century ago, those interested in self-defence arts in Europe were considered primitive exotics who meet in their hallowed halls to prove their strength to each other with wild shouts and strange movements. In real dangerous situations, however, neither acoustic nor optical factors play a central role. The term "self-defence" is often used today for advertising purposes, although what is offered is unfortunately all too often the exact opposite. What is missing in this area is professional information. Even if it sounds a bit blasé for some, the term "self-defence" has lost its meaning today due to years of practised amateurishness, and it is time for clarification. The art of self-defence is so diverse and rich in knowledge. Art and science meet here. By adhering to physical laws and striving to perfect movement sequences, a completely new sense of reality emerges, which strengthens consciousness and allows us to see many things with a clear self-image that has been previously hidden.

Defending yourself requires knowledge and skill. The ability to use your own body correctly at the right moment and to function intuitively, is the goal of intensive self-defence training. As soon as tournaments, sparring and championships as well as conditional high-performance or acrobatics are mentioned, the topic is already tarnished and missed by miles, because self-defence has nothing to do with any of that.

At the time when I was still practising martial arts as a sport, "self-defence" was just a term that (as already mentioned) was widely used, but its meaning only became clear to me years later. Quite the opposite of reality, I had to devote myself to the club's internal attack and defence techniques and the associated regulations. The coaches were outraged when I questioned one technique or another. I had so many questions, such as: Why don't women fight against men at the championships? Why do they sort and differentiate by weight class in competitions, when what you train should always work, regardless of the physical condition and gender of the opponent? Why, the over-40s, who have 20+ years of training behind them, brimming with confidence, who should be the stars of every fighting team are now treasurers, chauffeurs of the fighting youth or temporary trainers? Does getting older mean you lose your skill and that is the end? Why can't a woman win against a man, or a lightweight man against a heavier man? If not, for what purpose are you actually training? What then is the point of martial arts? Is there one?

Of course, there is a reason to train in sportive martial arts. There are many martial arts with historical backgrounds. I support these martial arts because they offer children, and young people in particular, and of course adults too, an excellent opportunity to develop their coordination and physical experience themselves.

Even though I'm writing a book about the art of self-defence, I'm very happy that my father (a Judo trainer) committed me to training martial arts at the age of five. Of course, back then I thought that I had better things to do on some days. Today, I know that it couldn't have made a better impression on me. To this day, I am grateful to my father for always being strong and guiding me. He wasn't one of those effeminate, emasculated fathers who ask their children what they would prefer and then let their children make decisions and thus lead the way. My father knew that he was responsible and had to make decisions, even if I had a different opinion as a child (hard to expect otherwise). I didn't appreciate that as a child, quite the opposite in fact. Gratitude didn't grow in me until many years later, but that gratitude stays with me for life.

Back to self-defence. Reality is everywhere, and by that, I mean the reality that any of us can face at any time. Through shouting, wild movements or through visual attractiveness such as for example a well-trained musculature, only unaware people can be impressed or even shy away. So, it's no use looking like Hulk or some other impressive cartoon character. It takes a little more than that to defend yourself. However, a naturally built body is sufficient for this, just as Mother Nature created it, with the necessary "mind" to control it.

With WingChun* the student gets to know a system that can be described as an aggressive forward defence. Here the defender becomes the attacker and takes the lead.

Which attack method our opponent uses cannot and must not matter even for a second. All that matters is the irrefutable certainty of whether or not you are in danger and need to defend yourself.

With a kind of distance, selection and collision training, the WingChun* student gets to know all conceivable constellations of a self-defence situation. By constantly repeating processes, the right movement is ground into every visual perception. This leads us to either a preparation for an attack or a defence. The aim is the fastest possible and, at the same time, correct decision. The preparation, our own decision to attack, or our defence initiated by our opponent's attack, is exactly what we call complete, linked coordination. This is precisely where further decisions begin to grow from the initial decision, which we call follow-up techniques. All of our limbs react simultaneously and independently with different movements. Information paths are minimized, and the reaction speed is increased exponentially. With well-thought-out techniques that are appropriate to the respective situation and, if necessary, sequential techniques, it is made impossible for the attacker to reposition himself. The above-mentioned opportunity of preparation deals with procedures before combat and is only possible if the combat distance has not yet been reached (more about that in later chapters). The beginning of a fight is always an attack or a defence. At best, the fight ends almost immediately or just a few seconds after it begins.

As long as there are no sporting wars, there will be no sporting self-defence either.

For this reason, we avoid sparring, competitions and their typical rules because in reality they would lead to drastic limitations in self-defence. However, due to pronounced body awareness and the constantly increasing responsibility of the trainees, there are no serious injuries during lessons.

Well-founded belief in one's own ability gives martial arts students recognizable self-confidence. What must not be missing under any circumstances is inner readiness. Namely, the willingness to use all conceivable means to protect your own health or the health of others.

Only those who feel this willingness have an inkling of the meaning and responsibility of the term "self-defence".

Being ready requires confidence in one's own abilities, and this trust can only be achieved through practice and ultimately believing in yourself.

b. Social Programming

Our social conscience forbids us from intentionally hurting someone. Even in dire need, we would not want to harm an attacker and would attempt to evade the situation in other ways. As long as we want to defend ourselves using rational thinking, we are in mortal danger. Every thought costs valuable, never-recurring time, which can have fatal consequences in any emergency situation.

What we need is a system that, on the one hand, is taught to us with scientific intelligence, but which we can ultimately only master through intensive training. In the interaction between mental power and body feeling, a connection must take place through the constant repetition of certain, above all, logical processes.

The system must neither be based on brute strength nor athletic requirements. Although technical, functional strength is increased during practice. We definitely train ourselves into an appropriate condition by repeating movement sequences. However, this strength and the conditioning mastered through functional movements are accessible to everyone, regardless of age and sex.

If we manage to function without giving too much of a role to the intellect and only recognizing a brutal attack for what it is, freeing us of all kinds of judgment, only then are we optimally prepared.

Our actions are ethically and morally justifiable, as they are not used for sporting reasons, but are triggered by a self-defence situation.

Is it ethically and morally acceptable for you not to be able to help another person in a scenario unfolding in front of you because of your lack of self-defence skills?

c. Self-Defence and Combat

Learning a self-defence system should never be confused with having fun fighting. The emergency situation where you have to defend yourself (your life) is no fun. This is a serious matter, namely protecting our health and our lives and, of course, the lives of others. When you practice real martial arts, you become a self-defence expert. This in no way means that you develop a love of fighting. Rather, you develop a love for perfection of movement and total control in all conceivable circumstances.

The primary purpose of the art of self-defence is to protect your health and life. As a secondary purpose, one could mention improved coordination skills and a strengthening of the tendons, ligaments and muscles. Ultimately, the primary and secondary purposes are to maintain and improve your health.

A martial arts instructor teaches the motor skills and physical capabilities that are available to a person to avert an attack as quickly as possible with the greatest level of protection, and to instantaneously start a counterattack. A martial arts instructor also teaches unconditional self-defence, which should be used solely for the purpose of self-protection. So, the fun of fighting is exactly the opposite of what you should learn if you are interested in self-defence.

d. Homo Sapiens Sapiens, how are we progressing?

I keep seeing combat styles that offer self-defence according to their advertising, but then don't even use the motor skills of our ancestor, Homo erectus (from the Latin erectus - upright, who lived around 1.85 to 0.3 million years ago). Instead, they prefer to move on the ground like reptiles in their martial arts.

I often heard the question at my seminars: "Can you show me a ground technique?" Quite a frequently asked question, arising from the belief that it would be sporty to drop down and then assume a "fighting position" while lying on the ground. Admittedly, these kinds of questions hardly surprise me anymore. The application of general information represents an extraordinary challenge for laypersons.

Wasn't it the circumstance for thousands of years that, in the best-case scenario, the loser ended up on the ground? What drives people in the 21st century to take such an evolutionary step backwards? No one can rule out falling or tumbling in a self-defence situation, so no doubt one does need to practice individual, useful, ground-situated emergency techniques from time to time, but does that mean we have to make this the best case or declare it to be absolute?

Homo sapiens sapiens is the scientific term for the anatomically modern human (homo - human, sapiens - clever, wise). All humans alive today belong to this species and are very closely related to each other. Since many paleoanthropologists assume a classification into different species, the term Homo sapiens is often used today without the addition of the subspecies.

Even if fights and battles were not among the wisest acts of mankind, they took place primarily in an upright position. The fact that some train fighting on the ground as the ultimate form of self-defence is still a mystery to me to this day. After all, in all historical writings, the losers were the unfortunate ones who ended up on the ground.

The Battle of Megiddo in 1468 BC (Egypt defeating Syria) is the first documented warfare, as confirmed by hieroglyphic writings in the Temple of Karnak and other Egyptian inscriptions. It was thanks to this battle, led by Thutmose III, 6th king of the 18th dynasty of Ancient Egypt, that Egypt rose to become a global power and became the first real-world empire.

What would the battle have been called in the history books if the warriors had behaved in the light of modern-day fighting?

"The Ground Battle of Megiddo"

Or what would we have called the clash between the warlords Alexander the Great (Greek side) and Darius III. (Persian side) in 333 BC.?

"333, The Big Crawling of Issus"

Please forgive me for this cynicism, but I just want to point out the misguided ways in relation to "single combat".

However, evolutionary retrogression can also be seen in many other areas. Look at all the things people do to weaken their upright posture. Under the name "Nordic Walking", instead of maintaining healthy back muscles with an upright gait, people instead choose to walk with crutches. Like their very early ancestors, they use their arms, now with the help of two sticks for locomotion, and they seriously believe that this type of primate-like movement is now a modern sport. This is totally insane. I can only marvel at the trends of our time. But whatever. These four-legged "athletes" don't harm anyone but themselves. The bad thing about it is that in the area of keeping the human body healthy, the interpretations and perspectives are becoming more and more disastrous, confusing and absurd.

Hence, the legitimate question: "how are we progressing?"

e. From Knowledge to Skill

Every skill requires learned knowledge. It makes no difference to our minds whether we physically implement our existing knowledge or not. However, regular stimulation is necessary so that the synapses created through learning and insight are not lost, as has been proven to be the case according to the latest findings. This would mean that memories and any skills associated with them would be incomplete or even deleted. A lot of what we experienced in the course of our lives and learned through seeing, hearing, smelling, tasting and feeling, but also emotional experiences, are to be found in our memories.

However, it is quite difficult for us to implement the knowledge we acquired years ago. We are all too often forced to ask questions to fill in the gaps that have arisen or to look up suitable reading material to refresh the knowledge that has been lost. The knowledge that we regularly use or physically apply can gradually become a skill that we use almost intuitively. We do something without seeming to think about it. Like seeing and reacting to a vehicle's brake lights ahead of us when driving and applying the brakes of the car in a conditioned response. Our brain implements the information developed through knowledge and especially through experience (repetition) without delay. We don't doubt our decision for a moment and put our foot on the brake pedal. We train our brain in this way in all imaginable situations, and especially in sports. For example, consider a table tennis tournament. Isn't it amazing how quickly a human brain calculates the trajectory of such a small ball and controls the player's hand holding the racket so precisely? You can admire the extremely fast and precise brain function and instant calculations made in a number of sports.

Especially in self-defence, it is important to immediately perceive a threat visually in order to be able to react without consideration processes, as is with a natural reflex.

A part of our brain (the thalamus) connects information that is perceived via our sense organs, like a post office. The only problem lies in recovering memories. The hippocampus is responsible for this, working in conjunction with the amygdala, which is responsible for feelings. For recovery, the brain needs reference information based on images, movements, feelings, smells, etc.

However, since reference and distraction stimuli are constantly being processed at the same time, a kind of filter system is required, such as searching for the colour red in a room. With this experiment, you can directly experience the filtering mechanism of your brain. The brain is an extremely efficient computer, reducing about 11 million bits of perception per second to only about 10 to 50 bits of consciousness.

We remember by reconstructing what we see, hear, and feel. Even with virtually incomplete information, our brain makes hypotheses about the further consequences. We finish an incomplete sentence or finish a partially recognized movement. The brain is in constant interaction with the body. Not only are we able to feel movement, we can even feel a colour. Feelings are constructive elements. A very specific scent can cause us to remember a specific positive or negative moment from our past. We are able to emotionally perceive a movement or, for example, an image.

The conscious and the unconscious being.

The brain needs about half a second to control an action. It takes about another half a second to realize it. This makes it clear that a reaction has little to do with a rational approach. The belief in rational deliberation processes is pure illusion. Perhaps this is also a clever human protective mechanism that does not deprive us of our possibilities and our higher intelligence, namely the subconscious intelligence that works faster and more precisely than our tangible intellect. Let's deal with the first half second. Since we do not consciously perceive this first half second, some explanations are necessary.

A second often elapses between the readiness and the actual self-initiated action.

The phenomenon of advance warning in the brain before an action begins is called the readiness potential

(Named by the two German Neurophysiologists Hans H. Kornhuber and Lüder Deecke, Brain potential changes in voluntary movements and passive movements of humans: readiness potential and reafferent potentials)

The brain prepares an action by calculating how best to carry it out. This readiness can be measured about half a second before the start of an action, before muscular activity. On average, the subjects of the neurophysiologists mentioned above started the readiness potential 0.55 seconds before the action but became aware only 0.2 seconds before the action. So, it took 0.35 seconds to consciously experience the decision.

Almost half a second after our brain begins preparing our decision, we become consciously aware that we want to perform an action that "we" have decided to do.

I will never forget a sentence from this treatise. Let it affect you and watch your thoughts.

"Not the consciousness, but unconscious processes are at the beginning. When a decision is made, the consciousness is not present".

(Hans H. Kornhuber and Lüder Deecke).

Of course, I read this paper not as a scientist but as a martial artist. For me, the interpretation was about when and to what extent I make conscious decisions in a situation in which I have to defend myself. I asked myself whether it is dangerous to take an action in the self-defence phase that you only consciously perceive as a decision 0.2 seconds before. The answer was immediately present: no! In the case of self-defence, it is more of a risk to consciously reconsider an action. There are instances of veto that enable us to reduce the effect of a movement or to change it through a kind of transitional action. After all, we have 0.2 seconds to object to the upcoming action before it takes place. The conscious mind constantly sorts out suggestions from the subconscious. Though consciousness cannot begin an action, it can interrupt it.

After reading this scientific paper, the word self-awareness took on a whole new meaning for me.

f. Talent is no Coincidence

Countless times have I heard the favourite excuse of resignation: "I'm not talented". It's so frighteningly easy to give up, especially when you've found such a seemingly valid reason. But someone or something must be to blame for our inability. An incredible number of people go through life with this attitude. And whenever something doesn't work out, you're either not talented, you've been cheated, treated badly, etc., blah blah. But stop! You alone are responsible for your life. Only you are responsible for your success and failure, and this applies to all areas.

How long does an athlete have to train before they say they are among the world's best? How many pictures does a painter have to paint before they are said to be talented and called an artist? How long does it take for a singer to become well-known and be called a star? Personally, I don't think all the world-class athletes, artists and stars practised and trained with the intention of being famous. Most of them practised humbly, perhaps simply because they loved what they were doing.

Presumably, a particular type of movement, which of course differs significantly from sport to sport, is easier for some people to learn than for others. Perhaps because of their physiology and/or their mental abilities, these people would find it easier to learn a certain type of sport or exercise. Unfortunately, it is a fact that those who are "gifted" rarely make the limelight. Maybe it's the lack of challenge. The first few weeks and months dedicated to the new hobby might have been too easy. For decades, I have seen how those who develop their skills with patience and determination will end up being the winners.

The difference between winners and losers is not the mistakes that are made, because all people make mistakes. The big difference is that winners get up and keep going, even when they fail, or it becomes extremely difficult to keep going.

g. The Way is the Goal

This sentence can hardly be surpassed in terms of simplicity and ingenuity.

We each go our own way. Whether it's the way you want to go or the way you go because you think you have to. Every decision, every action moves us further on our individual path. In our fast-moving times, many people find it very difficult to commit to their path. Hardly anyone takes the time to define their own life, to be clear about what they really want and where they want to go. Almost every day, we feel compelled to make compromises and thus distance ourselves from ourselves, little by little. Most compromises are exactly the opposite of what we actually want or need. In other words, something that fundamentally diverts us from our path and withholds the necessary insights from us. We become puppets of others, often without realizing it.

Of course, as an individual part of the whole, it is necessary to consider the needs of others in order to ensure social coexistence. I can't counter that in the slightest. However, we shouldn't lose sight of our way or even march blindly in the wrong direction. Certainly, this would lead to the impasse of helplessness and the pursuit of pseudo-goals (set by society or by certain individuals). Some of these goals are mostly material goods that we run after like sheep in the hope that one day they will give us the answer to the meaning of (our own) life. But far from it, they create strangely more and more dissatisfaction.

The physicist W. Heisenberg once said, *"Today's world has lost its orientation because mankind has surrounded itself too much with its own technology, and the old compass provided by nature can no longer function."*

(Werner Karl Heisenberg)

One thing you should never forget: This is YOUR life, and not a single day will ever repeat itself. The meaning of life is that you do what you want to do. What you would do if certain circumstances arose is irrelevant.

The real wealth is your health and life itself.

All questioning ends with the acceptance that the meaning of life is within myself. I get the answers from the inner depths of my being as soon as I allow it. Realize that happiness and unhappiness are contrasting experiences. Unhappiness belongs to happiness, like darkness to light and cold to warmth. By admitting these facts, a completely new dimension arises. Reaching this dimension is called freedom.

Consider the meaning of life as the encounter with your own centre.

In Taoism, it is said: "The way is the goal."

If you manage to go your own way, you have already reached your goal.

Stick to your path, and you will live an interesting and happy life. Enjoy each new day with the satisfaction of being true to yourself. Make your life decisions with confidence.

Paradoxically, goal setting is now practised as a kind of sport. I keep hearing that you have to set this or that goal, and so people follow those goals that others have suggested. That is absurd. In their private and professional lives, millions of people are under the misconception that they have to accept the individual goals of others. So-called motivational trainers, I call them "slick talkers," simply sell their opinion and their goals to others and earn their salaries by persistently talking about some kind of goal suitable for the masses. That's smart, but it's not good, except for the "slick talkers" themselves. Of course, this never leads to success for the participants, but most people like to be told success stories and love to dream of their own success. In doing so, stimulated by their own imagination and the tenacity of the "slick talkers," they often enter into the most impossible deals and then achieve less than if they had never listened to them.

If "goal" is equal to "way," then searching for goals is nothing more than searching for the way. Once you have found your way, you can finally stop setting yourself new, unsuitable goals that do not match your own path. Happy people don't need goals set by others. According to the law of attraction, those who have found their way will find those who accompany them on this path.

h. Freedom through Ability

Martial arts promote your own strengths and sharpen your perception. Martial arts potentiate visual and motor intelligence. The creative ability to process what is seen as quickly as possible (also emotionally) is increased. Only those who are aware of their abilities and know their possibilities can use them with self-confidence. Anyone who learns a martial art gets to know themselves better. Traditional martial art transforms you into a humble and purposeful person. Follow this Science of inner growth, as it will lead you on the path to a relaxed, free, conscious and healthy life. Accept the intellectual challenge and find the bridge between body and mind.

III. History and Terminology

a. History and Origin of WingChun*

Before presenting my source research to you, I would like to start with a little research on the history of China.

After the Hemudu (over 5000 BC), the Yangshao, the Longshan and the Liangzhu Cultures (until about 2200 BC), the dynasties of Chinese history followed: the Xia Dynasty (2070 to 1600 BC), the Shang Dynasty, also known as the Yin (1711 to 1066 BC) and the Zhou Dynasty (1066 to 256 BC).

The Chin Dynasty (221 to 206 BC): In 221 BC, The Chin Empire occupied the entire territory from the north-eastern border and united the warring states of China into a single empire. In the West, this is how today's name China came into being.

The Han Dynasty (206 BC to 220 AD): From the Han epoch come documents and scrolls with detailed descriptions of the human energy system. Instructions on Qi Gong exercises as physical therapy to cure illnesses and descriptions of the function of diaphragmatic breathing were created.

Insights into the central importance of the human energy system as the key to health and longevity stem from this period.

A period of political turmoil and rapid social change followed the fall of the Han Dynasty. The period of the three kingdoms ensued; the San Guo Dynasty (220 to 280), the Jin Dynasty (265 to 420) and the period of the northern and southern dynasties, Nanbei Chao (420 to 589).

During the Southern Liang Dynasty (502 to 557), an old Buddhist monk came to China from India. His name was Bodhidharma. The Chinese called him Damo. After years of meditation, he began teaching monks at a monastery how to strengthen their bodies for higher spiritual practices. He taught Chinese martial artists to use mental abilities to improve their respective martial arts. Damo brought martial arts and meditation together in a single exercise system, triggering a shift in martial arts training in China. Damo became the founder and father of Chan Buddhism, a combination of elements from Chinese Taoism and Tantric Buddhism. This is the form of Buddhism that later spread to Korea and Japan and became known as Zen Buddhism. The result of Damo's teachings were amazing warrior monks and spiritual martial artists, an unprecedented Buddhist and Taoist scene in China. Here is a sentence from the writings of Damo:

"It is of the utmost importance to seek motion in stillness and stillness in motion, and thus move incessantly until one attains the exalted state."

(Bodhidharma)

The exalted state could mean many things, such as spiritual awareness, emotional balance, physical vitality, or perfect health.

The Sui Dynasty (581 to 618) and the Tang Dynasty (618 to 906) followed China's golden age with almost 300 years of cultural flowering. The ancient imperial city of Changan became an open-minded, cosmopolitan centre with the finest artists, architects, scientists and scholars of all persuasions. The art of printing and gunpowder were invented and porcelain technology was highly refined. The Tang Dynasty was probably the most fruitful era for Taoism. After the dynasty failed due to the hunger for power of its regional rulers, 50 years of turmoil and war resulted, with five dynasties and ten kingdoms (907 to 960).

Only the Sung Dynasty (960 to 1279) brought unity and allowed the arts to flourish again. Porcelain making and landscape painting were among the highly valued arts. Confucianism, after Kong Fuzi – known in Latin as Confucius, 551 to 497 BC. whose significant influence on Chinese culture was not recognized until long after his death, was rediscovered. In 1026, Wang Wei Yi invented the famous "brass man," which is still used today in acupuncture as a model for the most vital meridians and points. The importance of Chi as a central factor in the treatment of disease spread during this period. The great war hero Yueh Fei created a system of Qi Gong exercises that is now known all over the world under the name "Eight Brocade Exercises." These exercises stimulate and balance the flow of energy throughout the body, stimulate the muscles, strengthen the tendons and loosen the joints. To this day, it remains one of the most effective exercise sequences in the entire Qi Gong repertoire. Yueh Fei was the founder of the Hsing Yi martial arts style that works with internal energy.

The downfall of the dynasty came when the Mongols of Genghis Khan and Kublai Khan stormed in from the north. After long attempts to infiltrate China from the north, Emperor Kublai succeeded in conquering all of China in 1279.

He established the Yuan Dynasty, a Mongolian Dynasty (translated Yuan means "primaeval beginning") from 1279 to 1368 and built a new capital called Dadu in the area of present-day Beijing. Marco Polo once reported on the glorious splendour of this city. A master of this Mongolian dynasty was Chang San Feng, the father of Tai Chi Chuan and the Qi Gong forms, which are still known and respected all over the world today. Chang was an excellent martial artist as well as a master of meditation. Chang was also a doctor and a learned Taoist philosopher.

After about 100 years, the Chinese rebels were finally able to end the foreign rule of the Yuan Dynasty and re-established a Chinese ruling house with the Ming Dynasty (明朝), 1368 to 1644 (please remember the character for Ming 明 for later). An era of cultural and economic prosperity began in China, similar to that of the Tang Dynasty. This was followed by territorial gains and the exchange of goods and ideas with the rest of the world. The Ming Dynasty is considered China's renaissance. There were trade routes to Arabia and Africa. A master named Tung Hai Chuan developed a martial art called Pa Kua Chang.

In 1644, the Ming Dynasty came to an end. Mismanagement and corruption among court officials and eunuchs led to the erosion of state power. That year, the last Ming emperor hung himself in a park when his country was not only divided by internal inadequacies but fell under the rule of the warlike Manchu people from the north.

The Manchu or Qing Dynasty ruled from 1644 to 1911. The capital was also located in what is now Beijing. The Qing Dynasty represented foreign rule again and, with 10 emperors in a row, was one of the longest and at the same time the last dynasty in China. Conquests took place in the West (including Tibet), but internally, China gradually began to stagnate. The last emperors did next to nothing to further develop or reform China. Many technical inventions failed to develop further in the 18th century. During this time, the Europeans made enormous technical advances.

The confrontation of Chinese culture with the highly armed Western imperial powers and their social theories heralded the end of dynasties and empires as early as the beginning of the 19th century.

Later the Republic of China (中华民国, Zhōnghuá mínguó, 1912 to 1949) and finally the People's Republic of China (中华人民共和国, Zhōnghuá rénmín gònghéguó since 1949) came into being.

After this brief insight into the history of China, I would now like to present my theory about the origin of WingChun*. Let's go back 380 years. With the fall of the Ming Dynasty (明朝), the country fell under foreign rule again.

Under the rule of the Manchus, isolated groups emerged that engaged in forlorn fights against them. The expulsion of the occupiers and consequently the recovery of the

Ming Dynasty was the only and supreme goal of these groups.

This required an art of war that, in contrast to the arts that had existed since then, could be learned very quickly and did not necessitate any time-consuming training. Only in this way was it possible to produce capable soldiers in the shortest possible time. After an extremely short training period, these soldiers were used against the Manchus.

Now, this assertion raises the legitimate question: could one learn WingChun* in just a few months? I would like to offer you a possible answer to this. Today's WingChun* cannot be compared in the slightest with the WingChun* that was being developed 380 years ago. A fighter from that era was estimated to be training about six hours a day, to cite a number. That would be about 2000 hours a year. Nowadays, a WingChun* student trains about three hours a week. If they train regularly, they clock up a mere 200 hours a year. A student back then could train almost as much in a month as a student today can in a year.

That's not a big deal, because the priorities for learning this art have changed drastically. In addition, it must be mentioned that WingChun* has been extremely reformed. Many masters over the generations have made it what it is today. At the same time, professional teaching systems have been developed by excellently trained instructors of various WingChun* styles, especially in the last 40 years.

But let's continue. As already mentioned, the Manchus invaded the country from the north. Many civilians fled to southern China. According to my research, WingChun* originated in the prefecture of Fatshan, which is in the province of Canton in southern China. Pirates threatened southern Canton as early as the Tang Dynasty. This may be one of the reasons for the excellent development of martial arts in the South. Interestingly, Taoist, Confucian and Buddhist principles were already being incorporated into the arts before the end of the Ming Dynasty. Even before the end of the Ming dynasty, adherents of different "faiths" were developing new styles together. The styles of the South were characterized by hand techniques and those of the North by leg techniques.

Wherever the Manchus occupied the land, they destroyed and burned the temples. Fleeing from the Manchus, a group from Fatshan who wanted to fight the Manchus gathered in a southern temple of Fukien Province in the Weng Chun District (永春县). They called their training room the "Hall of Eternal Spring" (永春堂, Weng Chun Tong).

Strictly speaking, our way of writing, with which we try to write a Chinese character in letters, is only a sound recognition. An official spelling would be the pinyin Romanization, but more on that later.

Yǒng would be e.g. the (Mandarin) pinying Romanization for Wing. However, I will omit spellings in the High Chinese Mandarin language, such as Yǒng Chūn for Wing Chun, in the following sections. I use the long-established and well-known expressions of the WingChun system, which have been passed on from generation to generation in the Cantonese dialect and Latinized.*

A renovation of the entire terminology is really not necessary. Because no matter how much we concern ourselves with the *dialects of the Chinese language, one thing is certain, however, we translate a Chinese character and write it with our Latin letters, the Chinese spelling is the same. The Chinese language uses only characters, and those who do not write or speak the language must somehow put down on paper what they understand. It is also not necessary to learn the Chinese language. WingChun* doesn't need any words in the true sense, because it's ultimately a martial art.*

I mention this because WingChun teachers are repeatedly asked for numerous names, which no doubt causes confusion these days. For example, if you were to use the spelling Yong Chun (and not Yǒng Chūn) and if you were to claim that it was standard Chinese, you would already have demonstrated half-knowledge before you started teaching the art. Because if it's in Mandarin, then please either use the characters 詠春, because that's Mandarin, or at least the pinying transcription Yǒng Chūn. If possible, the explanation that Yǒng is pronounced in the third tone, falling-rising and Chūn in the first tone, consistently high. I am very sure that in the end, the name would be the only thing that one as a creator would change in this chaos anyway. So far, I have not been told about a change in the entire technical terms of a WingChun* style (into Mandarin). But the spirit of invention knows no bounds and meanwhile, I even hear more and more grotesque stories of origin. Starting from a "battle nun" to a kind of Chinese "druid master".*

My following historical explanation is only the result of my very personal research. I found support from one of my senior students from the USA, whose native language is Chinese. Certainly, there is research that leads to different understandings, but perhaps there are also those that led to similar results as I have. Since I'm not one of those people who accept without questioning what is written, I did my own research. It would be optimal to compare and link different research, as each of us can easily have overlooked something.

From here on, only the simplified spelling of the original Cantonese dialect is used. As mentioned above, WingChun was born in the province of Fatshan but did not have this name at the time of its birth or for some time afterwards. The Cantonese dialect was spoken in the province of Fatshan at the time WingChun* was created. As a European, using this simplified spelling ultimately makes pronunciation easier for me. The characters used later serve to complete the historical background and are added purely for information. Say the words in bold next to the characters as if you were reading an English word, so we have no problems understanding each other around the world. Further comments on the pronunciation would lead us past the actual topic.*

My father was a judo coach in the first league, but he couldn't speak Japanese. He only spoke the names of the techniques as he learned it himself or as it were written in the corresponding literature. I strongly suspect that in the decades of his work, he was not once asked about the correct pronunciation of a technique. Correct for him was simply the way he said it and passed it on. It was always about training and preparing his students for the fights. As a child, at the age of five, I already took part in my father's training. We all repeated what we heard, but most of all we tried to get the techniques right. My father was an excellent and well-known judoka because he was above all a diligent and practical man and did not theorize everything.

To complete this chapter, I enlisted the help of one of my students, as I only learned a little Chinese myself. The motivation to interpret, write, speak and understand some characters arose after my research when I revised the terminology and was shocked to find that one or the other technique was used in an adversarial way. As a traditionalist, I felt compelled to get to the bottom of the matter.

The development of my system took around ten years to complete (1997 to 2007). All of the techniques, forms and sections were renewed and improved with everything linked together. It must have been a tough time for my assistants who accompanied me during this time, as I was constantly coming up with improvements and modified versions of the techniques, especially in the first five to six years (until the founding of the IAW). Anyone who stood by me as an assistant during this time deserves my respect to this day.

Now on with the history of the origins of WingChun*.

We stopped at the Hall of Eternal Spring

永 (**Weng** / everlasting),

春 (**Chun** / springtime) and

堂 (**Tong** / hall).

The Radical

言 (**Jin** / to talk) came later to the character...

永 (**Weng**) and changed it to today's character...

詠 (**Wing** / to praise).

This should serve as a reminder of the way the art was passed on.

The system was only passed down verbally.

The verbal transmission and physical contact were necessary for the master (師傅 / **Sifu**) to initiate his apprentice (徒弟 / **Todai**) into the art of WingChun*. In the actual sense, the two syllables **Weng** (later Wing) and **Chun** mean nothing other than "eternal spring". This fitted in perfectly with this newly born art, which aimed to recapture the Ming Dynasty. What they wanted to express with the name of this art, without actually saying it, was therefore "eternal Ming Dynasty" (永明代 / Weng Ming Doi), the heyday (the spring) of China, which they wished would return. The modification of the character **Weng** to **Wing** is probably one of the most interesting aspects of the style's history.

Due to the historical aspects described, we at the International Academy of WingChun proudly use the calligraphy of the characters:

The secret greeting has prevailed to this day. At the beginning and at the end of each WingChun* lesson, those present (the teachers to all students and the students back to the teachers) symbolize the characters 日 (Sun, with the right fist) and 月 (Moon, with the left open hand). Interestingly, putting these two symbols together results in the character 明 (Ming, the dynasty).

Basically, also a symbol for the principle of permanently complementing polarity (Yin and Yang).

In this old traditional greeting and farewell, which follows a small bow, family cohesion is demonstrated. This greeting is considered a symbol of freedom, loyalty and compensatory justice.

日 (Sun) 月 (Moon) **明 (Ming)**

But now I would like to go into other radicals and characters that found their place in the history of WingChun*.

In lore, one occasionally finds the additional character 嚴 (**Jim** / strict; urgent; serious), which interestingly has almost the same expression as the radical 言 (**Jin** / to talk). In the first few years, this pointed to the secret tradition of WingChun*. Putting the characters Jim and Jin together (嚴言) could be interpreted as "confidential words". If you swap the radicals of the later character 詠 (Wing), you get 永言 (**Weng Jin** / always verbally), which probably meant nothing more than a reference to the verbal transmission of the style. This once again refers to the secrecy that one tried to hide cleverly and excluded any kind of written record.

I think that combining the character 嚴 (**Jim**) with the characters 永春 (Weng Chun) meant 嚴永春 (**Jim Weng Chun** / secret everlasting spring, or better yet, **Secret Everlasting Ming**).

Spring is a symbol of China's prosperous age, the Ming Dynasty (明朝).

In order to emphasize the effect and meaning of the characters as they were used some 380 years ago, I have no choice but to resort occasionally to a connotative translation of the syllables (radicals). This is the only way you can feel the fascination of the history of our self-defence art or, even better, our art of war.

But since, as mentioned above, the semantic, classifying radical 言 (Jin) and the phonetic component 永 (Weng), the two parts of the character 詠 (Wing), already drew attention to the secrecy. Later, when 詠 (Wing) was written, the suffix 嚴 (Jim) was dropped and the art had a new name. That is why the system of the International Academy of WingChun only contains the characters Wing and Chun, in one word **WingChun**. Two Chinese characters are now merged into an inseparable, single word.

To reiterate. Wing and Chun are just possible spellings of the two characters. In this case, there is no right or wrong when it comes to Latinization.

If you look closely at the history of the origins of today's WingChun*, you will find many more characters.

五枚 (**Ng Mui** / five roots; five tree trunks):

I suspect that 五枚 (**Ng Mui**) may well have been one of the art's first names, if only briefly. It was not until the following years that the name 永春 (**Weng Chun**)/ 嚴永春 (**Jim Weng Chun**) was used and finally the art received the name 詠春 (**WingChun**), which is still used today. With the possible first name or the appearance of the characters 五枚 (**Ng Mui**) the origin of WingChun* is pointed out.

This coincides with my assumption that WingChun* arose from five different systems. There were three unarmed martial arts masters (recall the martial arts mentioned in the history that might provide a possible choice) and two weapon martial arts masters (Lok Dim Buen Gwan and Bat Zam Dou). In the "emergency" a whole new system was created through the cooperation of these masters. After a short time, there was hardly any connection with the actual roots. A completely new style, WingChun*, was born.

Even today, the two weapon arts, Lok Dim Buen Gwan (Long Pole) and Bat Zam Dou (Double Knives) are taught in many styles of WingChun. Significantly the arts involved in its creation bear no resemblance to today's WingChun* styles. Through generations of masterful work, art has developed into what it is today. Today's development of the weapon arts Lok Dim Buen Gwan and Bat Zam Dou is absolutely irrelevant for an advanced student of WingChun* and yet fragments of these two arts are taught to advanced students of various WingChun* styles. Unfortunately, an aspect that is quite influential historically is often presented as "the high techniques" of WingChun*, but at the same time, it is not recognized or mentioned where these techniques can be found in the unarmed system of WingChun*.*

I hope to be able to clear up this almost embarrassing misunderstanding at this point and in a later chapter. In order to learn the evolved art, we must remain in the here and now. Let's trust our predecessors and their development work. Each master reformed and shaped the art based on their skills, experience and character traits. By practising these old forms, we get at best a small excursion into the history of our style, but nothing more.

Just as I was researching the true meaning and naming of our techniques and the history of the origins of WingChun*, I learned the two weapon forms that, as explained above, should no longer be taught because they are just a meaningless aspect of the history of origins. So, what should one do once one learns and understands the weapon forms? Maybe what I did - to review and reform everything. I could quickly see that there were significant gaps and misunderstandings in the interpretation of the techniques. Since the weapon arts and their applications in my system already live on or have been brought back to life in the weaponless defence and attack techniques, my students train the techniques from day one like a master of other systems actually does immediately after learning them of the weapons arts would have to understand and implement. However, the question arises as to whether, after more than ten years of training (whilst learning the weapons arts and their applications), someone has the guts to throw the techniques they have been practising overboard and to redesign them - provided one recognizes the connection.

When someone teaches or learns the historical weapon arts (Lok Dim Buen Gwan and Bat Zam Dou), they should be aware that these arts only played a role in the development of WingChun*. Their functional movements must be found in the weaponless techniques of their current system. Neither the instructor nor the student benefits from training these historical movement patterns in isolation.

If what was involved in the development cannot be found in what already exists, then one can speak of a paradoxical situation.

If you train something, you also have to know why, i.e. keep an eye on the goal or the result of the training.

b. The Servant's Family Tree

I deliberately do without one of these 詠春 family trees, which often form the main part in other books. Who learned from whom, and who in turn learned from whom? The arithmetic game is best played ten or more generations back. If I imagine how many masters there must have been in the past 380 years, producing new masters, I can use a simple exponential calculation to determine that there should be hundreds of genealogical trees. Perhaps many people are attracted to the mystical unknown. You can tell a lot about people who no longer exist. We know absolutely nothing about the oddities of those who appear in this memoir. Not even their existence is certain. Students learn a family tree that they must memorize and repeat. The myriad of family trees serve no purpose other than to make the students believe they have found the right thing, the true thing, and the only way. Many who report on their "martial arts" pedigree are (and I'm sure they are) not even able to identify their own family pedigree three or four generations back. Who of us knows the name of their great-great-grandfather and knows about his life or profession? Wouldn't that actually be much more interesting?

Orient yourself to the living and don't follow any myths. When learning a martial art, you primarily require your own personal motivation and a good Teacher, 師兄 / Sihing (male) or 師姊 / Sije (female), nothing more.

History teaches us many things. Past events always arouse my interest. While I am lovingly retracing the origin and evolution of the Art of Combat, there is only one way to go, and that is forward. The history is a part of the whole and I respect it as such. But without going further, there would be no development. Reformations are taking place in all sorts of areas, and where would we be today without them? The opposite of evolution is stagnation and regression.

c. Everything has an Origin

In many arts, the reason for a regressive development can be found in the problem of the worship of myths. Over the years, I have had the privilege of getting to know quite a few masters of various martial arts on my countless journeys. I recognized early on this characteristic worship of bygone times and the associated search for the true path. If there is a way, nothing would be truer than to follow it (further), otherwise, the very beginning would be called into question. Every Grandmaster must primarily represent their style and not that of their many predecessors. Development is required here. What I was able to experience, on the other hand, was the opposite, namely the search for the truth in the past. And no matter how often I hear "Everything was better back then", the question "what?" still arises. Let's go back to the early Middle Ages. Hardly anyone lived to be older than 35, every second child did not even live to see their seventh birthday and child-birth was rarely survived, to name some of the most shocking facts.

The origin of our beloved martial art is now about 380 years old. It is grotesque to observe how today's "masters" pay more attention to old films or drawings by their deceased predecessors than to their own vocation.

What would Karl Friedrich Benz, who developed the two-stroke internal combustion engine in 1878/79, say if he could witness today's development of combustion engines? How would Alexander Graham Bell, who developed the telephone into a usable system in 1876, react to the development of mobile telephony today? And what about Thomas Alva Edison, who lit a carbon filament light bulb for more than 40 hours in 1879? Do you think that one of these ingenious inventors of their time could still contribute something to the further development of their technology today, after about 150 years? Would these gentlemen even recognize their inventions?

Respect and gratitude for the achievements of those who dared to take the first steps. The study of history is undoubtedly necessary for defining what was and is our identity. However, we must not forget one thing; We live in the 21st century, a historically interesting age, and that is far from the end.

I bow with respect to my predecessors and follow the path.

d. WingChun Terminology

In the terminology of the International Academy of WingChun, you will find the column with the traditional Chinese characters on the left. Next to it is the divided column for the English part: on the left the English phonetics of the Latinized syllables spoken in the Cantonese dialect (notation) and on the right the translation of the respective characters (translation). Here the denotative, but also partly connotative translation of the characters is used (such as the term "arm" in the translation of the character for "hand" to express the actual function).

As previously mentioned, it is the Chinese language converted into Latin characters in the Cantonese dialect. The pronunciation of the characters is therefore not to be understood in the Beijing dialect (Standard Chinese, also Mandarin Chinese and called Pŭtōnghuà by the Chinese). The pinyin transcription was not used here either. This simplifies the pronunciation for us.

In Chinese grammar, there is no declension, no conjugation and no cases, meaning the words are not changed. The grammatical function is determined by a large number of particles and by word order. Verbs often become adjectives through the described technical function and through the combination with a following character. This gives the WingChun* student a logical understanding of the application of the techniques. Of course, this functional understanding is only developed when the movements are learned.

INTERNATIONAL ACADEMY OF WINGCHUN

Glossary of Terminology

Chinese	English	
	NOTATION	TRANSLATION

拳套	Kuen Tou	Fist Set
標指	Biu Jee	Darting Fingers
木人樁	Mok Yan Jang	Wooden Person Pile
小念頭	Siu Nim Tau	Small Intention
尋橋	Tsum Kiu	Seeking Bridge

理論	Lei Lun	Theory
子午線	Zi Ng Sien	Meridian Line
針對線	Zom Doi Sien	Direction Line

手法	Sao Fat	Arm, Hand Method
擺指	Bai Jee	Swaying Fingers
標指手	Biu Jee Sao	Darting Fingers
膀手	Bong Sao	Winging Arm
黐手	Chi Sao	Adhering Arms
穿橋	Chuen Kiu	Piercing Bridge
大車輪手	Dae Che Lun Sao	Big Wagon Wheeling Arms
盪手	Dong Sao	Swinging Arm
拂手	Fat Sao	Whisking Arm
伏手	Fok Sao	Subduing Arm
撳手	Gam Sao	Pressing Arm
挭手	Gan Sao	Dividing Arm
搆手	Gau Sao	Dragging Arm
過手	Guo Sao	Passing Arms
滾手	Gwan Sao	Rotating Arms

刮手	Gwat Sao	Scraping Arm
圈割手	Huen Got Sao	Circling Slicing Hand
圈手	Huen Sao	Circling Hand
截橋	Jeet Kiu	Intercepting Bridge
擒拿手	Kam Na Sao	Grappling Hand
橋手	Kiu Sao	Bridging Arm
攔手	Lan Sao	Obstructing Arm
擸手	Lap Sao	Pulling Hand
甩手	Lat Sao	Casting Arms
問手	Man Sao	Inquiring Arm
破中落	Po Jong Lo	Breaking Middle Descent
盤手	Puen Sao	Coiling Arms
殺頸手	Sat Geng Sao	Killing Neck Hand
提手	Tai Sao	Lifting Arm
攤手	Tan Sao	Spreading Arm
托手	Tok Sao	Towing Arm
沈手	Tsam Sao	Sinking Arm
鏟手	Tsan Sao	Spading Hand
脫手	Tuet Sao	Releasing Arms
護手	Wu Sao	Protecting Arm
窒手	Zat Sao	Suppressing Arm

掌法	Jeung Fat	Palm Method
低平掌	Dai Ping Jeung	Low Parallel Palm
反掌	Fan Jeung	Reverse Palm
拍掌	Pak Jeung	Slapping Palm
抱排掌	Pou Pai Jeung	Embracing Tablet Palms
豎掌	Seu Jeung	Upright Palm
橫掌	Wang Jeung	Horizontal Palm

拳法	Kuen Fat	Fist, Punch Method
鈎拮拳	Au Git Kuen	Hooking Antagonistic Punch
寸拳	Chuen Kuen	Inch Punch
低平拳	Dai Ping Kuen	Low Parallel Punch
反拮拳	Fan Git Kuen	Reverse Antagonistic Punch
高平拳	Go Ping Kuen	High Parallel Punch
連環拳	Lin Wan Kuen	Linking Punches
外滾拳	Ngoi Gwan Kuen	Outer Rotating Punch
外衝拳	Ngoi Tsong Kuen	Outer Thrusting Punch
內滾拳	Noi Gwan Kuen	Inner Rotating Punch
內衝拳	Noi Tsong Kuen	Inner Thrusting Punch
雙拳	Seung Kuen	Double Punches
彈拳	Taan Kuen	Springing Punch
抬拳	Toi Kuen	Raising Punch
抬拮拳	Toi Git Kuen	Raising Antagonistic Punch
衝拳	Tsong Kuen	Thrusting Punch

肘法	Tsang Fat	Elbow Method
跪肘	Gwai Tsang	Kneeling Elbow
扱肘	Kap Tsang	Bowing Elbow
批肘	Pai Tsang	Hacking Elbow
收肘	Sau Tsang	Withdrawing Elbow

馬	Ma	Stance
正身馬	Jing San Ma	Frontal Body Stance
轉馬	Juen Ma	Revolving Stance
移馬	Yi Ma	Shifting Stance
側身馬	Zak San Ma	Side Body Stance
子午馬	Zi Ng Ma	Meridian Stance

腳法	Gerk Fat	Leg, Kick Method
膀腳	Bong Gerk	Winging Leg
斜撐腳	Che Zang Gerk	Slant Propelling Kick
圈腳	Huen Gerk	Circling Leg
正撐腳	Jing Zang Gerk	Frontal Propelling Kick
橫撐腳	Wang Zang Gerk	Horizontal Propelling Kick
拍腳	Pak Gerk	Slapping Leg
入腳	Yap Gerk	Entering Leg

步法	Bo Fat	Step Method
斜角步	Che Gok Bo	Slant Angling Steps
踏步	Dap Bo	Striding Step
交叉步	Gao Tsa Bo	Crossing Step
圈步	Huen Bo	Circling Step
箭步	Jin Bo	Arrow Step
轉步	Juen Bo	Revolving Step
上步	Soeng Bo	Advancing Step
樞步	Su Bo	Pivoting Step
橫步	Wang Bo	Horizontal Step

IV. Art and Science of Self-Defence

a. Art

I like to call WingChun* as well as the modern S.A.T, which includes the entire system, a "Self-Defence Art". One of the reasons is the unconditional distancing from sportive martial arts.

Parents enrol their children in a martial arts club, thinking their little ones will learn how to defend themselves. This inspiration probably arose from the fact that variations of punches and kicks are being trained. The assumption that punching, kicking and blocking etc. generally has something to do with self-defence seems a bit naive at first glance. The attacker also wants to kick and punch, as well as those who would like to defend themselves. Well, anyone can kick and punch, or learn to do it very quickly, but that doesn't necessarily make the movement you learn suitable for self-defence, and not everyone who can kick and punch is automatically a martial artist or instructor in the art of self-defence. Only a very small proportion of those who can kick a ball, ultimately become professional football players. There must be more to it than moving a fist or a foot forward, and everyone must realize that.

Many good martial artists, and occasionally their trainers, have lost sight of the actual sporting purpose and the original beauty of their martial art and attempt to offer their martial art as self-defence. This confusion can hardly be overlooked. Even street thugs now offer their beatings as a form of self-defence. They try to show those who were once their victim (because of the ruffians own physical superiority and limited social skills), how they could defend themselves against a similar situation next time. Anyone who does well in the schoolyard or on the street is far from being a master in the art of self-defence. Anyone who wears a black belt in a martial art can defend themselves against a street thug in the very rarest of cases. Defining the art of self-defence is a great challenge.

I can guarantee that the level of information regarding the art of self-defence or the art of combat will change systematically by the end of this book, especially for lay people.

The art of combat must be learned from the ground up. Learning this art will gradually increase your chances of being able to defend yourself against experienced attackers. Will, diligence, patience, self-confidence and study time play a major role.

The term "art" really has different meanings that elude definition due to complex associations. What art refers to and what artists deal with has changed significantly over time. There are various ways of approaching the term. However, the question arises as to how and in what context art should be defined. Art usually deals with perception, design, communication and inner, outer, subjective or objective reality. The term designates the aesthetic or artistic expression, as well as the creative expressions of the human spirit, and is used in connection with pronounced skills.

WingChun* and S.A.T are purposeful movement arts. Only perfect coordination helps us, especially in an emergency, to control our own body precisely, without unnecessary movements. In a self-defence situation, your own safety comes first. The attention is entirely on the selection of the most effective protection and control movements in connection with effective, consistent and at the same time secure attack techniques. The objective is to stop an attack and launch a counterattack within seconds, all without endangering yourself. The precision of the movements are therefore of importance.

The meaning here lies in self-defence, in the defence of health and life.

Coordination and application training keeps us healthy and constantly trains our brain with new requirements and learning programs. The art of body control, the control of movement, is our "sport".

b. Science

Science creates knowledge in a methodically controlled manner that can be understood and verified by any expert in every detail, anywhere, and at any time. This goes beyond ordinary everyday knowledge, that knowledge which is based on more or less limited experience and intuition.

Science is generally unbiased as to the result and not dogmatic. Unfalsifiable theories are unscientific. Science forces research, and research creates progress. Research supports, refutes, or refines existing theories. Scepticism in the sense of a critical attitude towards one's own results and theses as well as those of others is an essential principle of science. The distinction between scientific knowledge, ideologies, and doctrinal claims is that the latter use subtle means of power to enforce claims, and questioning is undesirable. Those who think differently are usually pacified by narrow-minded advertising slogans, unfounded claims or, if that is not enough, by slander. Scientific knowledge can be checked, at least in principle, by anyone using their own intelligence and experience. As long as a theory is not falsified, it can be considered preliminary scientific knowledge.

For these reasons, I refer to WingChun* and S.A.T as scientific arts. All movement and functional patterns can be learnt by anyone at any time and can therefore be technically checked after a short preparation time. The difference to well-known science is the reference to one's own body, which plays the main role in checking a movement pattern. Body and mind form a unit, which supports results and thesis, even if only partial success is achieved physically due to initial lack of coordination. Intellectually, we are aware of the fact that our ability, and therefore our understanding, grows through constant repetition. Because of this fact, I hesitated for a long time to write a book about a self-defence art. Despite my love for the art of self-defence, everything that is written is only theory. But then again, exactly this thought-provoking impulse inspired me. Because how else, if not through written or verbal and, above all, professional clarification, could an interest in something that is partially unknown or possibly been conveyed incorrectly arise?

V. Action or Re-Action

Since we can't fool our subconscious, I doubt there's any technical difference between action and reaction. As we already know, every action is a reaction to a sense perception. We often refer to a response to an action as a reaction.

In self-defence, waiting (hesitation) has long been recognized as a problem. Every second we waste waiting, our own thoughts lead us to rational decisions. We start evaluating, rethinking, and struggling with fears and uncertainty. The result is indecisiveness.

Now some might object that in a self-defence situation, it might be better to wait, as we force the attacker to make a conscious decision. We could then take advantage of an action taken in the subconscious, which would be faster than the conscious, and rationally brought about decision.

Here is the thing; there is no conscious choice here. Every decision takes place in the subconscious. It doesn't matter whether it comes from the attacker or the defender. The only question is which of the two is better prepared or trained for their action or reaction. The person who initiates the action can also be forced to react if, for example, the situation is reversed due to an error and the attacker is suddenly the one being attacked.

The worst mistakes for a martial arts practitioner in a threatening situation would be:

- Waiting too long, especially at a dangerous distance. This happens when the intellect mistrusts the subconscious and constantly doubts the newly learned skills, i.e. keeps objecting to what our brain calculates.

- Assess whether the attacker wants to attack with the right or left arm, or other irrelevant facts that you cannot change. Ratio and analysis can quickly work against you to your detriment. The worst thing you can do to your subconscious is to constantly object and doubt everything.

- Changing a certain position (stance) several times in the hope that it would be the right one for the expected attack. The attacker will hardly wait until his opponent has finished his picture-perfect defence preparation.

- One thinks only of defence and suppresses the possibility of going on the offensive themselves.

By the way: since the word "self-defence" does not contain the word "attack", an unbelievable number of people, even after months of training, think they have to defend themselves first and only then are they allowed to attack, i.e. fight back. The fact that one's own attack is already the defence against an impending attack does not seem to be taken into account at first. Here too, the intellect deceives us by believing it understands what has been read without having looked at it from all angles. They think they know something because they have read a word. This is a phenomenon that has been observed for a long time.

With the thought of having to wait (model defence against model attack), the entire system and, analogously, the entire training would be called into question. Our attack, even if we characterize it as a counterattack or as an act of self-defence, is what advanced martial artists deal with. There is a difference between taking your opponent's every attack seriously with a defence, or instead degrading it to insignificance with a counterattack that protects you. Don't take your counterpart too seriously and maintain a healthy indifference in a (to your mind) threatening situation. If someone wants to attack you, that doesn't mean that they can implement their wish technically.

Whether a decision is made consciously or subconsciously is ultimately irrelevant, because it is made within us. The words conscious and subconscious do not change the fact that the action is trained by ourselves and for whatever reason. The result of diligent training, insight, confidence and experience is accessed and executed by ourselves at the right time. It doesn't matter whether we can understand it intellectually or not. First and foremost, it must work.

Consistently develop realistic confidence in your abilities.

VI. Economy in Motion

A defensive situation can and should only last a few seconds. The goal of every martial arts professional is to end an unwanted confrontation as quickly as possible. We deal with the art of quick victory and after a relatively short training period, we have the best prerequisites for it.

The economy and thus the optimal coordination of all movements used frees us: from unnecessary use of strength, from physical weaknesses and from risk of time working against us. We do not allow the attacker a second chance due to delayed perception or hesitation.

Our goal is the immediate, direct attack that leaves no time to think. Consistent technical processes, controlled by our eyes, are taught.

We work to use our muscular system in such a way that we move exactly those muscles or muscle chains that are needed for a specific process. This allows us to focus on what is actually happening and what needs to be primarily dealt with. At the same time, this skill saves us unnecessary tension and time-consuming relaxation actions and ultimately conditional labyrinths.

Every year I appreciate martial arts more. It allows me to use my body more and more economically and to achieve the greatest possible success with the simplest of movements. What you thought was impossible when you were young, or rejected because of your almost limitless energy, suddenly becomes fascinating.

WingChun* is an art that offers us the possibility of endless development of our own skills, regardless of the age and condition of the user. Centuries ago, this fact made WingChun* one of the most extraordinary martial arts in history.

VII. Collision, the only solution

If the fighting exercise merely begins with a touch on the arms of the training partner and the attack does not hit the body as planned, or at least collides with a defence, there was no real attack and consequently no real beginning.

Those who neglect the importance of the beginning do not learn to fight.

After my article "Let's Collide", which I published ten years ago, I received countless e-mails asking why I talk about collisions in our style and what exactly I mean by that. In many e-mails, I am also asked for my opinion on sparring. I will deal with both topics briefly.

Many organizations were established just to create new associations with elaborate new logos, but technically everything stayed the same, whatever the old was or what was left of it. These selfish desires can hardly be called innovations. The cause of today's complications in the scene were numerous new labels with confused content that was partially compiled from various systems.

a. Sparring

Sparring for a traditional combat art can never be seriously considered. It is impossible to measure true self-defence ability in sparring, especially when wearing protective gloves and expecting both opponents to exit the practice field largely unscathed. It is not permitted to wear practice gloves during WingChun* lessons, as this would enormously impair the substance of the techniques and their effectiveness. Training gloves serve to protect the opponent. However, the attacker is hardly responsible for protecting his opponent. The opposite is true in the art of war. Only your own protection is of interest, nothing else. We defend ourselves with our hands and arms, and we attack without protective gear. Protection is based on ability, not equipment.

Anyone who wants to practice WingChun* with sporty sparring definitely has a considerable deficit in terms of understanding or assessing what is a game and what is reality. The use of the forearms and elbows for defence and attack would have to be ruled out when wearing gloves, which is absolutely impossible in WingChun*. Anyone who only uses fists in WingChun* so that sparring can be practised must listen deeply to themselves and ask themselves whether WingChun* (respectively the art of war) is what they actually want to learn.

Sparring is trained in sportive martial arts, to which this exercise method fits due to the technical repertoire. Sparring is an absolutely necessary practice variant of many martial arts and there is nothing wrong with that. However, I have never heard of students from these martial arts training the Chi Sao of WingChun* to strengthen their arms and/or incorporating the WingChun* forms to increase body tension and coordination. So why should WingChun* students enjoy sportive martial arts exercises? This makes no sense at all and just shows how confused and ignorant many are.

WingChun* and S.A.T lessons are hard training and relate to unmistakable reality. Sparring has nothing to do with reality. It definitely is a practice method for several martial arts, but not for WingChun*. I suspect that many martial arts instructors, unable to provide validation for their students, resort to martial arts sparring exercises to make their students feel strong once in a while, even if it means sacrificing essential and effective techniques. This suggests a pathetic training program and the incompetence of the WingChun* instructor. You can't and shouldn't play with real weapons because you lose sight of the essentials.

We should not change the original art to a sportive and ineffective, playful version.

The essence remains unconditional victory, which must be practised.

b. The Collision

Attacking with the intent to hit will inevitably result in a collision with the opponent's body or defence.

In the case of a punch, for example, either the fist hits the target or the attack collides with the defence of the attacked, there is no other possibility.

Now, an extremely large number of what I call "contemporary fighters" believe they can somehow neutralize an opponent's attack with various nonsensical methods. Some wish to "steal" an opponent's power, others talk about "borrowing" the power, and then there are those who "yield" and want to gently, redirect an attack. They begin their so-called sensitivity training by touching their arms, which is absurd. The mistake lies in misjudging the beginning of a fight.

Combat training always begins before touch, and so-called touch or contact is merely the end of an attack, namely a collision.

Thus, there is no touch "in the sense of a gentle contact", but only the inexorable end of a movement. It is reasonable to assume that many use the word martial "art" in reference to their style to avoid demanding training and its indispensable efforts. They simply use the term "**art**" and have ousted the wholeness of its understanding.

To believe that single combat begins with a touch and to assume that one can still react correctly after this touch, is almost schizophrenic.

This trained perception disorder arises when you train over a longer period of time in a homogeneous community and start where the real struggle ends. You make it easy on yourself and practice tactile constellations that would never occur in a real fight. Of course, this saves you hard and realistic training, but there is no unencumbered touch. If you start the training by contacting the arms of the other person, you are doing nothing. I trained this way many decades ago, as there was nothing else available at that time. It took me many years to realise that these training methods just wasted my time as they are never found in real combat, and this had to change immediately.

Attack and defence do not begin but end with contact.

What is important is what you do before and after contact, i.e. before and after a collision. As already mentioned, the collision inevitably occurs when attack and defence meet. The resulting contact with the arms or legs confirms an intact defence. Only those who are well-trained and stable enough to survive an attack can initiate their own attack.

Training the sense of touch is nonsensical and has nothing to do with the art of war. But the confusion has its source. For some time, there have been some who offer to learn their entire system in just a few weeks. Anyone who can show off their system in a few weeks is just saying, "I don't know much, but I'm happy to share it with you." Such bleak offers aren't worth dwelling on. However, that and much more, which I will explicitly detail in a later chapter (XVI Dream Factories), led to today's dilemma. A kind of hippie culture emerged in the scene (Peace - we are all the same). Highly motivated students lose valuable time since the existence of these dream factories.

We are not all the same.

Some learn faster, others slower, some train more, others less. Then some learn the wrong thing but are highly motivated. Others, who are learning the right thing but are bored by the teacher's essential explanations, consequently lose attention and wait impatiently until they can continue, but with the same mistakes. We live in an absolutely crazy world. As a motivated and interested newcomer to the scene, it is extremely difficult to find the right teacher and, above all, the right style. I have to openly acknowledge this fact.

VIII. The Elementary Basic Techniques

a. The 12 most important techniques of the system:

- **Two Stances**
- **Two Steps**
- **Two Pre-Positions** and the Meridian Line
- **Two Attack Techniques**
- **Two Defence Techniques**
- **Two Combination Techniques**

This and the following chapter serve as a routine check for all WingChun* students and instructors in particular. Instructors train their students regardless of their own preferences because what is neglected to teach at the beginning of martial arts training is difficult to make up for. The following 12 techniques are essential and require full attention in the first few weeks and months of study. Mastery of these techniques enables the student to build upon and gradually complete the system. There are no shortcuts or other ways.

Building the foundation of a large building takes a lot of time. As work begins on the foundation, we see nothing of the building and can only vaguely imagine the end result. If we have a picture or a plan, it is easier to imagine. If someone describes the picture or the plan to us with their understanding, it is more difficult to imagine. Once the tedious work is completed and the foundation is laid, work on the construction of the building can begin. Time and time again, I was amazed at how quickly things progressed as soon as the foundations were completed, after watching the construction of various new buildings during a daily drive. For months, there was not much more to see than busy builders and heavy machinery, but then, out of the blue, the first floors appeared and were completed within weeks.

If you are a student of WingChun, check your foundation with this chapter and with the following chapter, as this is the first and most important work of the building. As an instructor, you will find it easy to follow my explanations in Chapters VIII and IX. It will merely be a repetition of what you have internalized for years. As a student, you should try to create a mental image of the building to be built.*

By mastering these 12 techniques, a WingChun* fighter can recognize and break the preparations of his opponent, defend against attacks and start his own attack. With just these 12 techniques, I could easily create a simple self-defence system that most people would use to go through life prepared and confident. In every martial art, the most essential thing always comes first, and this is also the case with these 12 Elementary Basic Techniques of WingChun*.

However, a martial artist striving for their ideal wants to learn more and develop the highest level of creative functionality, flexibility and fighting power. A skilled martial artist must be prepared for anything. For an honourable martial artist, there is no "done", no "I already know everything", no "that's enough for now" and no "I don't have time". A martial artist who walks the path of the master does not cultivate these destructive phrases, rather, they despise them. A martial artist lives, loves, walks, acts, eats, sleeps, works, trains and thinks like a martial artist. This condition manifests in disciplined behaviour with the knowledge that there can never be enough.

You must maintain and, if possible, improve the skills you have learnt. Statements such as, "I used to be able to ...", "I used to know ...", and, "I used to be ..." do not exist for a master or a master aspirant. A master is better today than yesterday, but would never be better yesterday than today. In the beginning, learning and understanding new techniques demanded full attention, later the demand lies in the repetition of what has already become second nature. Whoever behaves in a masterly manner becomes and remains a master. Nothing pleases me more than recognizing and naming a master, for only in this way will the truth be passed on.

The way of the master starts with the right attitude, and the master is made who keeps it.

The following information on the details of the techniques in their distances (centimetres/inches/feet) and description of the angles will act as a guide. They serve to understand the beginning, the function, and the end of a movement. The techniques described on distances and angles vary slightly depending on body size or arm and leg length. This information is intended to be of assistance only. No one checks a step or technique with a ruler or protractor. WingChun* lives through flexibility and individuality. Nevertheless, points of reference in the form of distances and angles are crucial to understand a technique and its dimension.

b. Two Stances

Stance 1 – Jing San Ma / Frontal Body Stance (called "Basic Stance")

A stance or posture is the foundation of every subsequent movement, and thus the beginning of everything. With correct posture, we are able to change and balance our weight and provide the stability we need to defend and attack. When attacking, we face the attacker head-on to maintain neutrality in the use of our body in relation to the reach of our arms. The shoulders lie on one coincident line with our feet in this stance. When the attacker enters a certain (main) distance, we are forced to leave this position to initiate our own attack. After or during an attack, as well as after or during a defence, all stances result in simple possibilities of moving in all directions. From each stance, there are a multitude of possible steps and after each step, we reach another stance. Changing from one stance to another is also one of the possibilities of WingChun* footwork.

We stand with the upper body straight, the knees slightly bent and the feet shoulder-width apart, measured from heel to heel about 50 cm (20"). The weight is evenly distributed on both legs. The hips are pushed forward, supported with a straight spine and the entire, upright upper body. The feet point inwards by about 15 degrees to ensure stability of the legs, providing a high level of flexibility.

A flexible way of compensating change would be, for example, the Juen Ma / Revolving Stance (called "Turn"). In "Basic Stance" (Jing San Ma), the knees point slightly forward and slightly inward under constant tension. The legs are in the form of a taut arch. Pressure is exerted forwards from the hips until a targeted tension of the entire body can be felt. The build-up of this tension is hardly recognizable visually because the upper body remains upright and straight in this position.

Under no circumstances should the knees be pressed too tightly together or even touching one another, otherwise the standing position would push backwards (in the wrong direction) and be extremely unstable.

Stance 2 - Zi Ng Ma / Meridian Stance (called "Fighting Stance")

Great attention is paid to this stance in the first few days and weeks of training. It allows the student to move forward efficiently and quickly. The main advantage lies in the very simple control of the legs.

The body's weight is positioned 80% on the back leg and is stabilised with constant tension on the front leg, which should not carry more than 20% of the body's weight. On the back leg, the foot points inwards by 15 degrees on an imaginary horizontal line. Equally, the foot of the front leg is also positioned 15 degrees inwards on an imaginary vertical line. If, for example, the right leg were in front, and it would rotate to the left, "inside", it would lead us to form the Jing San Ma stance.

The distance between the feet (in Zi Ng Ma), measured from heel to heel, is about 40 cm (16"). Since the body is kept straight with slightly bent knees, there is only the mentioned, visually imperceptible weight distribution over the front leg.

This bodyweight position is important to allow movement in the direction of the pressure described above (forwards). The weight of the body is carried and moved by the back leg. Meanwhile, the front foot acts as a brake. This makes moving forward quite easy, as you only need to lift your front foot off the ground. Lifting the front foot (releasing the brake), will result in our body shooting forward. By combining this action with the force of the back leg, we can move forward with speed and power.

Note a common mistake: The weight must not rest on the back leg without forward pressure, because that would remove the load from the front foot and make it impossible to move forward quickly. The tension must therefore be built up while standing, before the step, in order to release or use it, with the step and then restored with the following stance. In principle, all stances and steps of WingChun* function in this way.

c. Two Steps

Step 1 – Jin Bo / Arrow Step

The "Arrow Step", executed from Jing San Ma, the Basic Stance. The so-called Arrow Step is performed by shifting the body weight from the Basic Stance. For example, if we shift our body weight to the left leg, the right leg is relieved of its load. Due to the previously described tension and the angle of the foot being turned slightly (15 degrees) inwards, the right leg springs forward, with a small arc inward (but mainly forwards). In this example, you could imagine standing with your feet on the back corners of an isosceles triangle, with a target of reaching the apex with your right foot. As your body accelerates forward, moved by the initial pressure release, it is slowed down as soon as the tip of the triangle is reached. Whilst the body moves forward about 30 cm (1'), the back foot is rotated and pulled inwards, stopping at a corresponding distance of about 40 cm (16") (measured from heel to heel) behind the front foot. During the formation of the new stance, catch your body weight and balance it accordingly. We are now standing inside the imaginary triangle, and we have reached the apex with our right foot. After the Arrow Step from the Basic Stance, we reach the Fighting Stance and have already combined the first three standing and stepping techniques.

Which leg we choose to perform the step depends on the arm techniques planned or currently being performed. The step should therefore be practised equally, intensively, alternating with both legs.

In many martial arts, leg technique means the various kicks. This is different in WingChun*. When we talk about leg technique, we mean principally the stance and stepping techniques. In WingChun*, leg techniques are always given the same attention as arm techniques, because without one, the other is of no value. We explicitly refer to kicks as kicking techniques.

Step 2 – Dap Bo / Striding Step (called "Front Step")

The Front Step is performed from Zi Ng Ma, the Fighting Stance. When moving from the fighting stance, the front foot is lifted off the ground and the body moves forward. The tension build-up is released and the whole body accelerates forward, straight and upright. As the body moves forward, the front foot stops our travel after about 30 cm (1'). From here, a few other combining stepping techniques would be possible if required. If no further step is necessary, after the Front Step (Dap Bo) we again reach Zi Ng Ma, the Fighting Stance.

Dap Bo gives us the opportunity to move forward seamlessly. As described at the beginning, the weight is pushed forward by the back leg with an upright posture without needing to shift the weight before moving. With merely the lift of the front foot, the body moves forward. In order to control the weight of your own body as quickly as possible, under no circumstances should you transfer it to the front foot, the step length is only about 30 cm (1').

Once you understand the distances of combat (discussed in Chapter X), you'll quickly understand that longer strides are rarely needed. In the whole system, there is only one single stepping method that allows us to cover a greater distance, the Gao Tsa Bo (called "Crossing Step"). Of course, there is also a stance in WingChun, the Yi Ma, which is referred to as a "Shifting Stance" and is used to shift the body weight onto the front leg and thus shortening the distance to the opponent. From standing in Zi Ng Ma, a step is not required to perform an attack using Yi Ma. In this stance, the entire body weight is briefly shifted to the front leg in order to cover the distance very quickly. However, this stance as well as the stepping technique (which can* *also be combined with each other) are irrelevant in basic training, since they are not used in common single combat. I only mention these two techniques to complete the explanation and to make it clear how important it is to train the elementary basic techniques because all other techniques build upon them.*

After the step, we intercept our weight in time and can build up the tension described at almost the same moment. This allows us quick control, flexibility in all directions and if necessary, a further step.

After the Front Step (including other steps such as Gao Tsa Bo, Jin Bo, Juen Bo, and Su Bo), we always reach the Fighting Stance. Now an exercise for you to try: From *Zi Ng Ma* move your body weight from the hips, over the knee, to the front foot until the weight is evenly distributed between both legs. At the same time, rotate the front foot and the body exactly 90 degrees inwards. We now find ourselves, after Juen Ma (Revolving Stance), in Jing San Ma posture, the Basic Stance. The basic techniques can be perfectly combined. The 90 degrees turn (Juen Ma) here simply serves to complete the elucidation.

d. **Two Pre-Positions** and the Meridian Line

Pre-positioning of the arms
- **Wu Sao** / Protecting Arm (called "Wu")
- **Man Sao** / Inquiring Arm (called "Man")
- Zi Ng Sien / Meridian Line

Before starting the defence, the arms form a flexible wedge in front of the upper body. One of the arms, Wu Sao, protects the body, with the wrist, a little less than a hand's length from the body (about 15 cm / 6"). The other arm, Man Sao, takes the front position with the wrist, a little less than two hand lengths from the body (about 30 cm / 12"). Both positions are located above the Zi Ng Sien (the "Meridian Line").

In Man Sao, the wrist rests on the inner ring of defence that connects the Short Distance and the Main Distance (more on this in Chapter X).

The hands are open, fingers lightly touching and pointing upward in Wu Sao, and upward and forward in Man Sao (at about 45 degrees). The wrists of both arms are in the middle of the body (Zi Ng Sien), at the level of the shoulder joints.

In Wu Sao, the elbow is slightly below the short ribs to protect the upper body, and in Man Sao, it is at the level of the short ribs. Wu Sao and Man Sao are interchangeable at any time. There is no primary or secondary arm here. In their movements, both arms are trained equally, so that we can adapt to all conceivable attacks without setting any priorities. This is an extremely important aspect, because even "just" believing in a stronger arm, which we would primarily use for an intended action, robs our subconscious of the opportunity for free decision-making, even after years of training.

When I write that the wrists of both arms are above the Zi Ng Sien, I naturally mean the direction of the Zi Ng Sien, the physical alignment with the opponent. I'm writing this again explicitly because there are those who think they have to fight at the height of the Meridian Line or protect the Meridian Line (also called the 'centre line' in many styles). Of course, that is not the case. Protecting just a line cannot be seriously considered in combat. Positioning Man Sao and Wu Sao too low does not guarantee your complete protection. To protect lower areas, i.e. solar plexus, there are techniques such as Gan Sao, but more on that later. The Meridian Line is an aligning or pointing element. The fight does not take place on but with the help of the Meridian Line. Think of the Meridian Line as a kind of energy ray that pierces from your solar plexus through the middle of the opponent's body.

In principle, the Meridian Line does not depend on the positions of the arms and exists in isolation. Even if an opponent were to strike both our arms outward, causing us to no longer occupy the centre, the Meridian Line will remain intact.

The Attack and Defence Techniques of WingChun lead forwards / downwards / outwards / inwards / rotating, from the outside forwards / rotating from the inside forwards / straight from the outside forwards / straight from the inside forwards / from up, sinking forward / from above, sinking down / from below, rising up / hooking, backwards, outwards and upwards, etc. For the possible bending of the Zi Ng Sien due to the situation, the necessary actions take place with the use of a technique from one of the three Tactical Systems (four forms) of WingChun*. In this case, one works with the principle of Zom Doi Sien, the Direction Line.*

Zi Ng Sien, the "Meridian Line", is not to be confused with Zom Doi Sien, the "Direction Line". In contrast to the "Direction Line", the "Meridian Line" cannot be changed. The "Meridian Line" grows from the middle of our body, starting with the so-called 7th joint, the spine, and forwards, at the level of the solar plexus. Traditionally, the spine is called a "joint" when it comes to the transmission of energy from the origin (we know however that from an anatomical understanding it is not a joint).

According to these traditions, the spine is the basic "joint", which is the first-rate "joint" for the transmission of power and for all techniques to be carried out. The seven joints of WingChun* are counted from the spine to the shoulder and elbow joint, to the wrist and further along to the smallest of the finger joints. Only those who know how to use stances and steps can transfer the power of the 7th "joint" to all other actual joints. It requires an understanding of Zi Ng Sien.

As an exercise you can easily check an accurate Zi Ng Sien (body and arm alignment). From any conceivable technical standing position in which you are facing your opponent, lock out your arms, and bring your hands together above the meridian line without any corrective movement of the upper body. If this is not the case, then Zi Ng Sien was clearly ignored, and you cannot, or only to a limited extent, transfer your available power into an Attack or Defence Technique.

As you attempt to perform the techniques mentioned later in the chapter, remember this control exercise. Zi Ng Sien focuses your power and drastically improves your technical execution. Zi Ng Sien maintains the equality of both arms, regardless of whether one arm is in action or not. This maintains your flexibility and ongoing control of the entire body as a unit, standing and moving. One of three Tactical Systems of WingChun* (explained in the next chapter under "20 Sections, four Forms and three Tactical

Systems") allows the Zi Ng Sien to be suspended, while activating Zom Doi Sien at a certain point in the execution of the techniques. I can recognise the level of a student by observing their understanding of the Zi Ng Sien.

Zi Ng Sien does not change direction and serves to align the body. It is the exact line on which Wu Sao and Man Sao are positioned in a neutral manner (Wu Sao remains adaptable to the right and left in contrast to Man Sao), usually initially when the opponent is not yet within either combat distance. The Direction Line, Zom Doi Sien and a variety of techniques logically do not have to maintain the direction of the Meridian Line.

In the example given (no combat distance, but preparation for a possible escalation), Man Sao, Wu Sao and the Direction Line point in the direction of the Meridian Line. This positioning is the classic beginning in WingChun*.

e. Two Attack Techniques

Attack Technique 1 – Tsong Kuen / Thrusting Punch (called "Punch")

Before we continue, here is an imperative piece of information about the WingChun* punch. The fist hits its target vertically. Rotating the fist during the punch into a horizontal position, would rob the rising elbow of power, forcing it to move outward, which in turn means that the slower chest muscles must counterbalance the direction of the punch. Using a horizontal fist has its own dangers. Since the knuckles of the fist, upon reaching its target, do not form a straight line with the forearm, the accelerated forearm thus works against one's wrist. This means that using horizontal punches, in reality, causes many injuries to the wrist. Anyone wanting to use horizontal punches in a real-life fight would need to bandage their wrist beforehand. This is done prudently in many sports.

Here is a small, self-explanatory exercise: Stand in front of a wall, stretch out your arm (elbow remains slightly bent) and first press the knuckles* of a vertical fist against the wall, and then rotate your fist to a horizontal position. Now observe the line from the bone of your forearm to the knuckles of your fist on both versions, and judge the line of force for yourself by slowly increasing the pressure. You'll find that you're more likely to injure yourself than your opponent with a horizontal punch. You'll also find that a vertical punch requires no corrective movement and even stabilizes the wrist during execution.

** Knuckles here means the Metacarpophalangeal Joints (MCP Joints) and the connected proximal phalanges of the fingers.*

In WingChun*, hitting with the fist is subject to accurate mechanics. We focus on Wu Sao position. Of course, this position can only be a snapshot of a movement. The Wu Sao position usually arises from a relaxed, hanging arm upon the recognition of a potential preparation to attack from an aggressor. Completely unprepared and, due to the distance from the aggressor, we immediately decide to prepare an attack (in this case a punch) as the first defensive measure. This creates the position "Wu Sao", which (especially if the main distance is reached) does not pause there, but will continue to execute a punch.

Let's freeze the image of Wu Sao for a moment. The wrist is a hand's length from the upper sternum, over the Zi Ng

Sien, in the centre of the body. The low-positioned elbow is only a few centimetres from the body, as it is the key joint for all techniques performed via the triceps. It is the joint that accelerates the forearm to attack or defend. If you hold your wrist in this position and let your arm hang completely relaxed, you can determine the optimal position of the elbow. The elbow is slightly below the lower short rib. This is very important and serves to protect the entire upper body, especially in the initial phase of the punch. From this position, if you pull your wrist straight forward in the middle of your body, you can visually perceive and mentally store the path of your elbow to perform a punch or assume the Man Sao position.

Now, you practice the entire sequence of the punch from the Wu Sao position. The decision to strike is reinforced by closing your hand into a fist and raising your elbow to accelerate the forearm. The wrist is used in a straight line to perform the Tsong Kuen. Of course, later in the system there are also rising, falling, low, hooking, double, high and rotating punches, which require more or less differentiated executions. The wrist remains locked throughout the punch and does not change position from Wu Sao through Man Sao to the completed punch. The full concentration is on the elbow, the power comes mainly from the triceps. The shoulders are pulled down slightly with the large back muscle (latissimus dorsi) and remain still throughout the execution. They are neither pulled backwards, raised up, nor pushed forwards. The stable shoulder joint is the basis for power transmission during a punch.

A little anecdote from my past. In the late 80s I was in Germany at a seminar of my Grandmaster, a student of Yip Man. The Grandmaster walked through the rows while practising the punch and checked the execution. He stopped at an instructor known to this day and told him to position himself properly and keep his shoulders back before punching. The shoulders were indeed pushed far forward and the improvement was justified. At that time, however, we all had enormous difficulties in executing effective (vertical) punches from this position due to years of practising various martial arts. However, the instructor has regrettably misunderstood that when hitting, he should pull his shoulders back.

Of course, if your shoulders are properly positioned, you don't need to retract them, and if they're not properly positioned, then you should retract them before the punch to first correct your posture.

From then on, this misunderstanding, namely the assumption that one should move the shoulders backwards when punching, spread like an evil spirit in quite a few WingChun styles. This led to a fatal error in the execution of the punch. When I asked my Grandmaster about this years later at a private lesson on the US West Coast, he just shook his head and told me that he hadn't brought up this posture error in years. He said that he preferred his students to have their shoulders pushed forward to perform the Tsong Kuen, instead of pulling the shoulders back while performing this Punch. He was misconstrued numerous times, requiring him to weigh the lesser of the two evils.*

I think he should have been more consistent with such a fundamental technique, but of course, I respect his decision. When managing errors, you can indeed weigh up whether you address them later and first stabilize the base. It also took me a long time to develop a concept for prioritizing transmission. If you want to correct everything at once, you can quickly digress from the most important thing. Above, I mentioned the locking of the wrist when punching, because misunderstandings and mystifications had spread here too. One common misconception is that when punching you should move your fist upwards with the use of your wrist, which is illogical. By the way, these were the same people who liked to train up to ten chain punches per second.

It would be so much fun to watch the movement of the wrist and the pull-back of the shoulder with every single punch in a sequence of say, about ten to twenty of these so-called chain punches in slo-mo. It would certainly be interesting to watch carefully and realise how far these grotesque ideas have strayed from reality and how they desperately try to hold on to their views. Since the essential knowledge has been forgotten, the martial art has evolved into an "artistic struggle" over the past three decades, but more on that in later chapters.

The fact that an attack can be a defence seems extremely odd to most who are new to self-defence. Only after a number of repetitions does it become clear how much one can devote oneself entirely to one's own execution and, after constant training, the would-be attacker no longer plays the role that was once assigned, with the fears that arose of nescience. The act of defending, which started out as a strange idea, becomes with practice commonplace, comparable to much of what we do in our daily lives. Of course, practising would be enough for us, and we would be happy if we were spared the day when we are challenged to apply this knowledge.

A real defence situation can never bring joy to a healthy and intelligent person. However, we know that there are not only good people, so ignoring reality and hoping for luck in avoidance would also be inappropriate for an intelligent person. We have little choice. Fatally, some imperative areas of knowledge are not taught in school. Knowledge of self-defence is one of these areas. If we want to lead a free and fulfilling life without fear, we have to acquire the missing areas of knowledge ourselves.

"If you want peace, prepare for war"

Supplementary exercise for:

Attack Technique 1 - **Lin Wan Kuen** / Linking Punches

The already discussed punch, Tsong Kuen, and the striking with two consecutive straight punches, Lin Wan Kuen are among the most relevant techniques of the system. This linking punch is listed and counted as a separate technique in the terminology, but there is no distinction in the execution of the individual punches. I consider Lin Wan Kuen to be an excellent motor exercise for detaching and fusing the processes needed. Therefore, I do not list Lin Wan Kuen as a separate technique in the elementary basic techniques but supplement this technique as an intense modification of Tsong Kuen.

One could compare these punches with arrows that shoot out of our body. This short series of punches, usually accompanied by a step, is what we call Lin Wan Kuen / Linking Punches. This means that we count a sequence of two punches as one technique. Executing a step from one of the two previously described stances gives the attack the necessary acceleration, followed and supported by the mass of the body moving forward.

When practising the sequence of punches, make sure that you punch straight until the arm is fully extended on a straight path at the level of the shoulder joints. This skill is trained intensively right from the start. The goal of the training is not just the hit, but the complete stretching of the arm and the timely link of the fists. From Wu Sao, the first punch of the Lin Wan Kuen is fulfilled. Man Sao lowers slightly to ensure the straight punch and makes its way back to immediately assume the Wu Sao position (with a closed fist), then punches forward as quickly as possible with the second, straight punch. Also, the completed first punch, like the Man Sao position before, sinks down a bit and moves back to take the Wu Sao position. This completes Lin Wan Kuen.

At the end of the execution, after the second punch, we move the outstretched arm back a little and finish the exercise with the Man Sao and Wu Sao positions. Now the hands are opened to underline the neutrality of the positioning. In this way, the musculature required for extending the arm and the correct release mechanism as well as the rapid return to the pre-positioning are trained.

The opening of the hands and the closing of the hands into a fist does not change the designation of the positions Wu Sao and Man Sao. Even closing the hand in only one of the two positions does not change the designation of the corresponding position. Rather, closing one or both hands into a fist represents a decision or preparation.

Of course, by improving your coordination over time, you would be able to do multiple punches in one second. However, one would focus on the number, not the optimization, of each punch. Start with two punches in a second, and if at any time you feel like you can do more, increase the power or decrease the time, but never increase the number of punches. This is how you train a short sequence of punches and force your muscles to coordinate perfectly. It's not about the number of punches, it's about their quality and effectiveness of landing one or two punches on target. To execute more than two punches decreases their effectiveness because if the first and second punch had been absorbed without effect, you would be wasting valuable time when it counts.

Important: Never punch more than a maximum of two punches for practice. It would be better to repeat this exercise countless times by alternating the pre-positions (Man and Wu). This is about the conscious, fast and powerful moving of the fists and not about the number of consecutive strikes.

If the first two punches in a real defensive situation are not successful, the next ones (however many) will certainly be even less so, because with a capable opponent, the fight would have been lost long ago.

Whether you need one or two punches, each must hit the target forcefully.

I myself know styles in which even advanced users hit countless punches, so-called chain punches, and thus twirl around in front of the supposed attacker. Even in demonstrations, the ineffectiveness of punching power is demonstrated by hitting an attacker over and over again. However, the opponent is not thrown away on the first, second, third or fourth hit, which should reveal to even the most inexperienced viewer that *something is very wrong here. Performers often don't realize how weak and clumsy they seem with their many attempts at hitting. They do it because that's how they have been taught and think it is part of WingChun*. I know that various styles are all about how many punches you can do in a second. In one second, with practice, it is quite possible to alternately "move your arms forward" at least ten times.*

If you repeat a punch that doesn't have any effect countless times because it's too weak, it will not get any better and, above all, it will not get any stronger. Here quantity is confused with quality, this is a fatal mistake in self-defence. Many sports and martial arts involve powerful movements. Examples such as in baseball - a powerful pitch, in tennis - a powerful serve, in javelin - a powerful throw, in soccer - a powerful kick, in high jump - a powerful take-off, these are to name just a few. The striking of more than two punches performed much too quickly, thus lacking power, is an unfortunate misunderstanding and renders a self-defence art useless.

There was once a method for practising Lin Wan Kuen's punch detachment and punch coordination. Lin Wan Kuen was simply repeated countless times. This exercise was eventually mistaken for a technique, leading to the disaster described above. The numerous repetitions of a technique, whether stepping, attacking or defending, always serve as an exercise. The error was mistaking an exercise for a technique. Today it is difficult to say why and when this obvious mistake was able to spread in WingChun.*

Returning to Lin Wan Kuen. With the exercise described above, you will soon be able to use one or two extremely effective punches during a defensive situation in about half of a second. With these first two strikes, you are certainly quicker than the reaction time of the opponent. As already discussed, we are not attackers here, but defenders. We react to an attack or its preparation and use the moment as the attacker is planning their attack, or is in the process of executing it. At this moment, it is almost impossible for the attacker to deflect both punches. If we start with a regular defence, we usually use a single punch as a follow-up technique. Train your punch until it has a destructive effect. To achieve this goal, you will find some of my helpful training guidance in Chapter XIII.

Attack Technique 2 – Go Ping Kuen / High Parallel Punch

As a point of reference for the execution of this technique, we take the position of Wu Sao, as is usually the case. At this point, I would like to mention that Wu Sao can be moved on a parallel line from the middle position to the right and left shoulder (distance from the body remains the same). This makes Wu Sao's protective position extremely flexible and offers us countless possibilities for defence and attack. Wu Sao stands exactly between the body and the inner ring of defence.

The two ways of positioning Wu Sao outside the centre are also called 'open' or 'closed' Wu positions. To perform Go Ping Kuen we use the open Wu position, that is, the one in which the wrist is brought towards the shoulder of the executing arm and positioned between the sternum and the shoulder.

To explain this technique, let's perform a right-hand side Go Ping Kuen. To achieve the Go Ping Kuen position, move your right Wu Sao to the described position, about 15 cm

(6") to the right. The wrist is still at the level of your shoulder joint. Now make a fist and move your elbow outwards and up until your fist is facing forward. During this movement, raise your fist slightly until the bottom of your fist is in line with the bottom of your chin and the elbow level with your shoulder. Now the wrist and elbow are almost at the same height. This is how you achieve the prepared position of a Go Ping Kuen. Go Ping Kuen is ideal for executing a punch that, after a Defence or Combination Technique (executed with the other arm), travels higher. Thus, it is not blocked by either your own or your opponent's positions on its way to the target.

f. Two Defence Techniques

Defence Technique 1 - Tan Sao / Spreading Arm (called "Tan")

The Defence Technique, Tan Sao, is one of the two most important defensive techniques in WingChun*. To explain in some more detail, let's recall the Wu Sao position again. Now, assume this position and rotate your palm to ensure that it is facing upwards as much as possible, while simultaneously moving your hand to the opposite shoulder. The middle of your forearm, measured from the Metacarpophalangeal Joints of the fingers to the elbow, is located at the centre of your body in front of your sternum. The wrist remains a hand's length away from the body and the elbow hanging low. This is the prepared position you assume before executing a Tan Sao movement.

Usually, you prepare the Defence Technique Tan Sao from the Man Sao position. Here you move back from the Man

Sao position; turning your palm up and finding the same position as described above, to form the Tan Sao preparation. When the prepared position of Tan Sao (from Man Sao) is reached, the Wu Sao position is pushed towards the body a little (about half the width of the forearm bone) by the front arm. The arms touch for a short time between preparation and action. The preparation of Tan Sao is not a final decision for defence but results from an optical, situational perception. This short-term Wu Sao and Tan Sao preparation combination, can be used as a defence (Tan Sao) or an attack with Tsong Kuen (from Wu Sao). If Tsong Kuen occurs due to the situation, the previous position of Tan Sao is abandoned (the arm is slightly lowered to clear the path of the punch). At the same time, during the punch (similar to the detachment of the arms in Lin Wan Kuen) it moves to a new Wu Sao position.

The Defence Technique Tan Sao is used to attack an attack, effectively stop an attack in its tracks. The opponent's strike is now stopped with the attacking Tan Sao or the opponent's body is attacked using Tsong Kuen, which we then characterize as defence (Tan) or attack (punch).

If one wants to perform Tan Sao correctly, the elbow accelerates the wrist a short distance of about 30 cm (1'), and the elbow itself moves forward only about 10 cm (4"), so the force passes through the stable position of the shoulder into the elbow and from there further to the wrist. The prepared forearm is at an angle of about 5 degrees from the body, and Tan Sao ends at an angle of about 45 degrees. Changing the angle is crucial in Tan Sao technique. The function of Tan Sao starts at the beginning of the arm movement and finishes just before reaching the end (about 30 cm / 1'). You cannot stop an attack with the Tan

Sao movement if it has not yet moved (prepared), or if it has already been completed.

The function of Tan Sao is to move forward. Tan Sao should not be initiated either too late nor too early.

In general, moving too early is out of the question, because if you had a time advantage, you wouldn't defend, but attack. Prolonged hesitation, leading to a motionless arm, and an incorrect elbow movement, are among the most common mistakes observed.

If you master Tan Sao, you can easily stop high attacks, which is where most attacks take place. The forearm, from wrist to elbow, has a length of about 30 cm (1') (varies by body size). Due to the forearm angle, which changes during the execution of the technique (angle becoming more acute), the defending functional area of your forearm decreases to about 20 cm (8"). As the functional angle changes, Tan Sao performed with the right arm (for example), protects the middle line of the body and also about 10 cm (4") of the left side of the body (if we are standing upright and straight in front of our attacker). The Tan Sao performed with the right arm, completely protects the right side, since Tan Sao can be used, not only forwards, but also to the slant angle, securing the side of the body of the leading arm.

There are two types of Tan Sao: the diagonal (crossing) Tan Sao, defending a frontal attack, i.e. carried out with the opponent's right arm with one's own right arm. The second type is a parallel Tan Sao, in which, for example one uses the right arm to defend an off-centre, left arm attack and vice versa. Using Tan Sao, we protect ourselves from high attacks in the centre of the body, as well as high attacks on the side of the executing arm. The head, neck and upper body are completely protected with Tan Sao. Tan Sao is a truly ingenious tool for self-defence.

As mentioned, a trained martial artist can successfully stop all high attacks with Tan Sao. It goes without saying that there are about 30 defence techniques in WingChun* for a reason. The entire repertoire includes techniques that would undoubtedly suit certain high attacks better than Tan Sao. Nonetheless, I state here that a well-trained martial artist could utilise Tan Sao for all higher defences.

I started my own experiment in the 90s to fend off all spontaneous attacks, even during demonstrations, exclusively with a Tan Sao. My senior students were amazed at this, and I sensed that they were trying to vary their Attack Techniques. But my attempt at that time to defend against the high attacks in general with Tan Sao worked excellently. After this experiment, I asked myself why I should not develop a simplified system with only two defensive techniques (one for high attacks and another for low attacks).

But this was only a thought that visited me briefly, then disappeared along with other fragmentary thoughts. In order to avoid risks, as a principled and tradition-conscious martial artist, one should want to learn and train the appropriate Defence Techniques. With certain attacks, which differ wildly in angle and position, there is always one method of defence that can be described as the most advantageous. Firstly, this ensures the highest possible level of security and, secondly, creates the best conditions for the ideal counterattack.

The Defence Technique Tan Sao (parallel) is optimally combined with the Attack Technique Tsong Kuen. The Defence Technique Tan Sao (diagonal) is optimally combined with the Attack Technique Go Ping Kuen. Together with the Stances, the Steps, the Defence Technique Tan Sao and the two Attack Techniques, you can now already combine some of the essential techniques of the system with each other.

Defence Technique 2 - Gan Sao / Dividing Arm (called "Gan")

Gan Sao is the technique used to defend against lower attacks. This is the second of the two most important defensive techniques. It covers attacks below the Tan Sao area, by which I mean attacks below the forearm (i.e. the line from wrist to elbow). The same applies when starting from Man Sao or Wu Sao preparatory position.

For low attacks, Gan Sao is the primary option, like Tan Sao for high attacks. If you master Tan Sao and Gan Sao, you are armed to defend against many variations of high and low attacks.

The preparation is similar to that of Tan Sao, but we distinguish the following for execution: To perform Tan Sao, after the palm has been turned upwards, the wrist is accelerated about 30 cm (1') forwards, but never downwards. To perform Gan Sao, beginning from the Wu position, rotate your palm to face your body and move your forearm across your body so that the forearm reaches the same preparatory position as is with Tan Sao. Then accelerate the wrist about 30 cm (1') down, but never forwards. The execution, even if it is directed downwards in Gan Sao, can definitely be compared to the movement of Tan Sao. However, the elbow hardly moves because it is already held down. When performing Gan Sao, the shoulder remains and stabilizes in exactly the same position as in Tan Sao.

With both techniques, at the end of the movement, i.e. to the collision (stopping the attack), the arm has covered a distance of about 5-25 cm (2-10"). When performing both techniques, the arm remains slightly bent at the end of the movement, even if you practise the techniques without stopping an attack you move about 30 cm (1') as a result. In both techniques, the acceleration comes primarily from the triceps, with the forearm bone colliding with the attack. Unlike Tan Sao, the muscles of the front shoulder cannot support the upper arm of Gan Sao during movement. In preparation for Gan Sao, time permitting, the elbow is raised a few centimetres in order to use the strength of the large back muscles when sinking (pressing down). The upper arm moves little or not at all when performing Gan Sao.

You can compare the Gan Sao movement to using a machete. Imagine chopping off a branch sticking out of the ground which is connected to its root with a machete. You would take a crouched but stable position and hit it with the front third of the blade to split the branch with only a few strokes. Advancing the blade would steal the power of the stroke and make it impossible to cut off the branch. Now imagine your forearm being the blade of this machete. You can use this visualization to perfect the execution of Gan Sao.

To use another analogy, imagine someone handing you a 40 kg (90 lbs) weight in the preparatory position of Gan Sao. Your arm would drop down. To train an effective Gan Sao, you should focus on the first 30 cm (1') of the direction in which your hand would move downward.

g. Two combination techniques

Combination Technique 1 - Pak Jeung / Slapping Palm (called "Pak")

Pak Jeung comes in two versions. Pak Jeung is usually moved forward from Wu Sao (open) position, but can also be moved backwards from Man Sao on rare occasions. In Pak Jeung from Wu Sao, the hand is positioned in front of the shoulder of the side of the executing arm, with the palm facing forward according to the setup of the opponent's arm. The movement thrusts forward diagonally and powerfully at an angle of about 45 degrees across the middle of the body, ending with a slightly bent arm. The power of Pak Jeung is transmitted through the movement of the low-lying elbow. Pak Jung is usually moved forward, and in some situations slightly downward.

Pak Jeung from Man Sao begins without further preparation from the Man Sao position (already in front) and is used to parry a core attack backwards and outwards, past your own shoulder. At the end of the movement, the elbow is about a hand's length in front of the centre of the body, the palm faces outwards and the thumb of the hand is in front of the shoulder.

Pak Jeung from Wu Sao is a technique that can be combined very well with Go Ping Kuen. An exception to the rule applies when executing Pak Jeung from Man Sao. In this case, the Wu position moves down due to the finishing position of Pak Jeung's forearm. Wu Sao becomes Tsong Kuen, who starts the strike at about the level of the solar plexus. Despite the slight incline, the execution mechanics of Tsong Kuen remain the same.

Pak Jeung from Wu Sao clears the way by slapping an opponent's arm out of the way with the palm. If the way to strike with the fist is blocked after using a diagonal Tan Sao, Pak Jeung is an optimal combination technique in this case.

To use an application example: An attacker strikes with their right arm. The defender, in Jing San Ma stance, stops the attack with the right arm, diagonal Tan Sao. The defender's left arm Wu Sao then prepares and performs Pak Sao. At the same time, the completed Tan Sao moves directly into Go Ping Kuen preparation and then execution, while the step Jin Bo is implemented at the same time as the punch.

With that we have the preparation Man Sao and Wu Sao, the defence Tan Sao (from Man Sao) the stance Jing San Ma (or Zi Ng Ma), a preparation Pak Sao (from Wu Sao) to move the arm of the opponent out of the way. Meanwhile shifting to prepare and execute Jin Bo or Dap Bo (step) and perform Go Ping Kuen (punch). Then immediately forming Zi Ng Ma (stance) and Man Sao, Wu Sao position after terminating the technical combination.

Now you have already linked eight techniques, namely two Stances, a Step, two Pre-Positions, a Defence Technique, an Attack Technique and a Combination Technique of the system.

To practice this, count 1-2-3. Count 1 = Tan Sao, 2 = Pak Sao, 3 = Jin Bo or Dap Bo with Go Ping Kuen, then immediately positioning Zi Ng Ma, Man Sao, Wu Sao. It shouldn't take you more than two seconds to perform this combination up to the executed punch.

Combination Technique 2 - Tsam Sao / Sinking Arm (called "Tsam")

Tsam Sao is used to slam your opponent's arm down with your own forearm. As with Pak Sao, Tsam Sao disrupts the preparation and positioning of the opponent's arms.

Tsam Sao can be prepared and performed from Wu Sao and Man Sao positions. The preparation of this technique is quite simple. From the Wu Sao or Man Sao positions, raise the forearm until it is almost perpendicular to the elbow. From this position, the forearm is struck forwards across the centre of the body, falling at an angle of about 45 degrees from the body. The execution is similar to chopping with an axe. The hand sinks (falls) down to the height of the elbow. At the end of the movement, the wrist is on the opposite side of the body at elbow height and the middle of the forearm crosses the middle of your body.

Here is an exercise for you: Prepare Man Sao (left) and Wu Sao (right) in Jing San Ma. Execute a left Tsam Sao from Man Sao hitting down the front, parallel (right) arm of the opponent, during which shift your stance to the left, preparing Jin Bo (right), then step forwards attacking with Tsong Kuen (from right Wu Sao). Immediately after executing this attack, form Zi Ng Ma together with the positions of Man Sao (right) and Wu Sao (left).

These basics and combinations, along with other valuable information, are taught in the first few weeks of study and perfected in the first year of training. They constitute the foundation on which we can build. The stances, the positioning of the arms, the basic techniques and some follow-up techniques represent enormous potential in martial arts. With the techniques described above, I detail to you what a WingChun* student should learn and practice in the first few weeks of training.

I have described here in words what I normally explain and demonstrate in a class in a very short space of time. For a long time, I considered whether I should describe these first techniques, the beginning, only in words without using image material. This is only intended to create a first feeling and can by no means replace the lessons. Here I want you to concentrate without visual aids, and first, mentally perform a stance or one of the arm and fist techniques. An image can quickly mislead, but the visualization leads to the thinking and feeling of each of the techniques described. By thinking about a technique, it becomes alive within us.

IX. The Technical Level of an Advanced Student

a. The 12 Additional Techniques

I will not fully explain the implementation of the techniques mentioned below, but will essentially name them.

With the level of education of an advanced student and that of an instructor, it is easy to understand this chapter. However, if you have just started training, you do not have to skip this chapter, on the contrary, after each quarter of training, you will understand more of what I am describing.

Those who are designated by their instructor as advanced students are initially characterized by their understanding and flawless application of the Elementary Basic Techniques. The syllabus is clearly defined, but it is still up to the student to improve their skills until they reach an advanced student level. This requires the motivation of the student and the professionalism of the instructor.

Advanced students who want to become an instructor or achieve a higher technical standard go through an additional technical level.

Personally, I only appoint an advanced student as an instructor once the 12 Elementary Basic Techniques have been mastered and the aspirant knows and is able to use at least four additional Attack Techniques, three additional

Defence Techniques and two additional Steps, two additional Stances and one additional Combination Technique.

An experienced WingChun* instructor therefore knows and is proficient in the following techniques, in addition to the **Elementary Basic Techniques**.

6 Attack Techniques:
Tsong Kuen, Go Ping Kuen + Noi Tsong Kuen, Ngoi Tsong Kuen, Noi Gwan Kuen, Ngoi Gwan Kuen

5 Defence Techniques:
Tan Sao, Gan Sao + Bong Sao, Gau Sao, Fok Sao

4 Steps:
Jin Bo, Dap Bo + Juen Bo, Su Bo

4 Stances:
Jing San Ma, Zi Ng Ma + Juen Ma, Zak San Ma

2 Pre-Positions:
Wu Sao, Man Sao

3 Combination Techniques:
Pak Sao, Tsam Sao + Lap Sao

This is now totals 24 techniques (12 Basic Techniques plus 12 Additional Techniques), which represents almost one-third of all techniques of the entire system. It should be noted that I do not like to count Lin Wan Kuen, which is declared as an exercise in Chapter XIII, as a separate technique, but consider it as a supplement to Tsong Kuen. Those who have learned to distinguish Tsong Kuen and Lin Wan Kuen and know how to apply the respective technique according to the situation, will enjoy an additional technical application. Accordingly, Lin Wan Kuen is justifiably listed separately in the glossary of terminology. Mastering these 24 techniques is essential for developing further techniques and thus reaching higher levels. In the execution and mostly even in the preparation of these techniques, every master can distinguish a beginner from an advanced student within seconds.

In the WingChun technician exams, I always evaluated the execution of these 24 techniques first. In order to check the implementation, there are numerous combinations of applications that I demanded of the aspirants. These combinations allowed me to check the simultaneous use of arm and leg techniques as well as the application of several related, complementary techniques as a whole. In the advanced tests, these 24 techniques should be fully understood and performed accurately. Correspondingly, the applications are demonstrated using the combinations learned. This allowed me to first check the status of a prospective technician and then decide whether to move on to the next level of testing.

For me, teaching these 24 techniques were always the main components when planning the Special Classes and the Professional Training Classes to become a WingChun Instructor.

Of course, an instructor should also know and be able to teach at least ten basic combinations (preferably a few more), such as:

- Jin Bo with Tsong Kuen or Lin Wan Kuen.
- Dap Bo or Su Bo with Tsong Kuen.

• Juen Ma from Zi Ng Ma with 90 degrees turn to Jing San Ma or 180 degrees turn to Zi Ng Ma with Tsong Kuen or Lin Wan Kuen when reaching the target position from Wu Sao (parallel and diagonal, depending on previous positioning by Wu Sao)

• Tan Sao (parallel) with Tsong Kuen (from stance with turn or step).

• Tan Sao (diagonal) – Pak Sao combination with Go Ping Kuen (from stance with turn or step).

• Pak Sao with Go Ping Kuen (from stance with turn or step).

• Tsam Sao with Tsong Kuen (from stance with turn or step).

• Gan Sao with Tsong Kuen (from stance with turn or step).

• Bong Sao – Fok Sao combination with a Tsong Kuen variant (from stance with turn or step).

• Tan Sao (diagonal) – Lap Sao combination with Tsong Kuen or Go Ping Kuen (from stance with turn or step), to name just ten imperative application exercises.

b. Lat Sao, Guo Sao and Chi Sao

Exercises such as Lat Sao (Casting Arms), Chi Sao (Adhering Arms) and Guo Sao (Passing Arms) are general WingChun* exercises and serve to incorporate concise techniques or technique sequences, which are used in combat to achieve the optimal attack position to quickly end a fight. In addition, these exercises serve to harden the forearm bones and, of course, to strengthen the tendons and ligaments of the entire arm and shoulder.

A defended self-initiated attack leads to a collision of at least two limbs. During a fight, we either attack or defend. When we execute an attack, we are conscious that in a real fight, the opponent could defend this attack; therefore, a collision is expected in reality. The collision with the opponent's arms should therefore be classified as unavoidable, and under no circumstances should the process be interrupted by the sensation of pain.

Those who avoid toughening up their arms during training are bound to fail in combat against brutal and callous opponents.

Lat Sao

Lat Sao is a structured combat training program. It is used by new students at the very beginning of their training and remains as an essential part for all advanced students. Lat Sao, initially consists of the movements Pak Sao and Go Ping Kuen. It serves to practice specially designed sequences, which in turn develop the understanding of the possibilities in the application of technical combinations. The integration of techniques such as Tan Sao, Lap Sao, Tsam Sao, Bong Sao, Fok Sao and all Tsong Kuen and Gwan Kuen variants, to name the most important, help the student to make the logical choice and practice switching between defence and attack.

There are three situational learning levels in Lat Sao:

- **The successful attack** which concludes a sequence

- **The repelled attack** and the use of a Combination Technique, which then again leads to a successful attack

- **The defence** and the successful counterattack (with or without a Combination Technique)

In combat, I am attacking, or I receive an attack. There are no more than these two possibilities in real combat, and therefore the same in training.

Guo Sao

The purpose of Guo Sao is to conquer and secure the centre. I used to refer to Guo Sao as "the struggle for the middle".

We employ a Bong Sao (from Wu Sao) to suppress a Tsong Kuen (from Wu Sao, starting from the middle of the opponent's body). A Fok Sao (from Wu Sao) is to change arms (to release) and to subdue the held position before performing the (usually inner) Tsong Kuen.

There are two versions of a Fok Sao. One arises from a parallel (external) contact with the opponent's arm, who has the intent to press to the outside. The other, for example in the exercise Guo Sao, has (diagonal) contact with the opponent's arm. In both situations, the Fok Sao has the intention to subdue and control the arm. The diagonal Fok Sao includes two rhythms, first, it moves forward to contact the opponent's arm and second, it slightly subdues the opponent's arm downwards. The elbow always remains below the wrist during this process.

Noi Tsong Kuen is an inside punch to break the opponent's rear Wu Sao position (on the Zi Ng Sien). Its target is to hit the opponent's midsection behind the rear protecting position. Our counterpart defends the inner (Noi) Tsong Kuen with Bong Sao (generated from the previously defended Tsong Kuen) which results in the Guo Sao exercise.

The same sequence (especially Bong Sao - Fok Sao - Tsong Kuen) can be used, as trained in the exercise, during an altercation.

The whole sequence then repeats and starts over, with the only difference being that now the Bong Sao is used to stop Noi Tsong Kuen. The exercise begun with Tsong Kuen, but during the flow, Noi Tsong Kuen is stopped using Bong Sao.

Chi Sao

Chi Sao and Guo Sao are excellent and indispensable exercises, which should not be excluded from the training for advanced students. Chi Sao serves both as a preparatory sequence of techniques for beginning the 20 sections of WingChun* and for students in basic training to stabilize the most important Basic Techniques. Together with Guo Sao, these two exercises strengthen the muscles, bones, ligaments and tendons.

In the following section, I explain the exact technical sequence (the process) of Chi Sao by reference to the technical segmentation of student 1 and student 2 (S1 and S2). Now imagine you are S1 and your counterpart S2.

The beginning:

S2 Tsong Kuen (preparation) - left arm/preparation from Wu Sao position

S1 Bong Sao - right arm - to suppress Tsong Kuen (which is still in the starting position)
S1 Ngoi Tsong Kuen - left arm - to attack from the outside towards the middle of S2's body

S2 Tan Sao - right arm - parallel outside, to defend against Ngoi Tsong Kuen (called "outside punch")

Here S1 and S2 reach a situation from which the Chi-Sao sequence continues without repeating the beginning as follows;

The Chi-Sao Sequence:

S1 From the position of the finished Ngoi Tsong Kuen - left arm - move from the outside position back to the Wu-Sao position to prepare Tsong Kuen (as at the beginning of the exercise).

S2 The Tan Sao follows the opponent's arm and switches to Bong Sao to prevent the prepared Tsong Kuen.

At the same time, the following scenario takes place with the other two arms:

S1 Bong Sao - right arm - moves outwards, forming Tan Sao to clear the way (here the middle) for Tsong Kuen of the left arm.

S2 From the position of the suppressed Tsong Kuen - left arm - moved outside by the Tan Sao creates Fok Sao – controlling S1's Tan Sao, then immediately attacks with Ngoi Tsong Kuen from the Fok Sao position, without breaking contact with the opponent's arm.

S1 Tan Sao - right arm - outside - prevents S2's Ngoi Tsong Kuen. Meanwhile, the stopped Tsong Kuen (in Wu Sao position) stays in contact with S2's (blocking) Bong Sao.

S2 Execute Ngoi Tsong Kuen again, now with a short Detachment of the position*.
S1 Tan Sao - right arm - outside - to repeatedly defend against S2's Ngoi Tson Kuen.

** Detachment of the position:*

Primarily, S1's Tan Sao has to apply pressure outwards to prevent S2's Ngoi Tsong Kuen.

Secondly, Tan Sao is not a preparatory attack position. The contact can be actively released by S2 for an immediate, renewed attack from the outside.

Thirdly, an attack from the outside cannot be stopped with an attack from the inside (here this is only a position generated due to a defence). An attack from an outside position must be given full attention and defended correctly.

Here (after the change of sides) the characteristic Chi-Sao Constellation would be reached. The sequence can now be started from the beginning or introduced as a continuing Chi-Sao Sequence, by S2 and S1 alternating. For teaching purposes, it is advisable to repeat the Chi-Sao sequence over a period of time and not count the number of repetitions.

We do not just move (or wiggle) our arms for no reason; both you and your partner have to understand the movements to generate the sequence correctly. Some of your movements are generated by your training partner, for example parallel Fok Sao, and some are generated by yourself and your own decision, for example Ngoi Tsong Kuen.

With Chi Sao, the understanding of a decision and a condition for attack or defence grows and makes it clear to the user that an attack or a defence cannot arise from all positions without further preparatory work or change. Chi Sao also trains the preparation of a technique with and without the contact of the opponent's arms. Chi Sao trains the perception of the main distance and neutralizes the preference for a technical position or arm. As well as the fact that Chi Sao serves to strengthen the muscles, bones, ligaments, and tendons of the body, it is one of the most valuable exercises in WingChun*.

c. 20 Sections, four Forms and three Tactical Systems

As an S.A.T student, you will not be confronted with sections and forms directly. The WingChun* student must learn these coherently and in a specific order in preparation for the respective graduation. This fact reduces the S.A.T students' training time to a minimum to achieve the highest combat ability. In S.A.T there is no separation between the tactical systems, since neither a sequence is observed nor a graduation is held. Like WingChun*, S.A.T is initially built upon the Elementary Basic Techniques, the Additional Techniques, as well as Lat Sao, Guo Sao and Chi Sao. In S.A.T the complete repertoire of WingChun* is taught without any specific order. In addition, essential weapons combat is included at the beginning of training. Since the S.A.T student does not have to prepare for gradings, instructors and students enjoy complete freedom in the material trained. The students remember what suits their level of education, i.e. what they are good at, and of course, they especially remember what they like because that is customarily the easiest to remember.

With WingChun*, a verifiable and categorical pattern is followed. By always teaching the Forms before the Sections, and by logically following the section levels, this small passage is extremely easy to understand for students who have already reached the first Section Level.

WingChun* includes three "Section levels", known as three Tactical Systems. The first level contains seven Sections for the combined training of the techniques of the Siu Nim Tao (1st Form) and the Tsum Kiu (2nd Form). The first two Forms of WingChun* together define the **1st Tactical System** and therefore merge with each other in the first seven Sections. The second level includes five Sections for combined training of the techniques of the Biu Jee (3rd Form), the **2nd Tactical System**. The third level contains eight sections for combined training of the techniques of Mok Yan Jang (4th Form), the **3rd Tactical System**.

Chi Gerk (remark)

Chi Gerk is not a Tactical System, although many like to refer to it as a Section, or sometimes as a Form. Rather, Chi Gerk is a method to train combined application possibilities of the legs (stances, steps, and kicks) and at the same time, stability and balance.

d. Summary and Notes

The whole system of WingChun* consists of 77 techniques. There are 56 techniques for the arms and 21 techniques for the legs. The names of the exercises, forms, and lines found in the terminology do not belong to the techniques of WingChun*.

- Out of 56 techniques for the arms, 28 are primary Attack Techniques and 28 are primary Defence Techniques (the Defence Techniques occasionally also include connection/combination techniques).

  I use the term "primary" because there are Attack Techniques that can be used for defence, and Defence Techniques that can be used as an attack in certain situations. Of the 28 Attack Techniques, 15 techniques are variants of a punch.

- Of the 21 techniques for the legs, nine are Stepping Techniques, five are Stances and seven are Kicking Techniques.

To make it easier, you can remember the following; WingChun* includes almost 80 techniques, of which around three-quarters relate to the use of the arms and around one-quarter to the use of the legs.

X. The Distances of Self-Defence

a. The Main Distance

The Main Distance (also called 1st Fighting Distance) is the key Fighting Distance of the system. It refers to the range that allows the primary use of the techniques of the arms (attacks and defences) and the legs (kicks). The Main Distance starts at a range of about 70 cm (2'4") from the centre of your body and ends at a range of about 30 cm (1').

In training, I call the longest range of the Main Distance, the **outer ring of defence,** which is decisive for the opening of the fight, and the **inner ring of defence,** the shortest range, where the transition to Short Distance is smooth. Imagine that both rings, the outer about 70 cm (2'4") and the inner about 30 cm (1'), surround your body like a kind of radar and regulate the use of the weapons respectively the selection of your techniques from the three Tactical Systems.

In combat, it does not matter how the opponent measures his own Main Distance, only your own assessment of distance, based on your own physique, is decisive.

The Main Distance is measured and checked in WingChun* exercises such as Chi Sao, Guo Sao and Lat Sao by touching your training partner's shoulders with the fingertips of both hands with your outstretched arms. If there is a difference in body size (usually also a difference in the length of the arms), the training partner with the longest arms is used as a guide. If the difference is significant, you can agree on a middle distance. With both options, you are in the optimal range. This would be exactly the beginning of the Main Distance (about 70 cm / 2'4"). Our opponent's punch cannot reach us at this distance unless the distance is shortened by one step. Which is why one would have to initiate at least a punch with a turn or step from Jing San Ma (or, starting from Zi Ng Ma, the already mentioned "Shifting Stance") to achieve a sufficient punching distance.

As long as the distance does not fall below 30 cm (1') the Main Distance remains relevant.

Incidentally, the infamous Chuen Kuen (called "Inch Punch") is practised and demonstrated from the shortest range of the Main Distance. The Chuen Kuen is struck from the Man Sao position. In order to position Man Sao correctly, the wrist is located approximately on the **inner ring of defence**.

After some time, advanced students can visually determine the distance and no longer require checks to assess the Main Distance.

In combat, you aim to end a conflict as soon as the Main Distance is reached. The greatest effect of most techniques unfold at this distance.

WingChun* training primarily relates to quickly reaching and operating in the Main Distance. Stepping techniques allow us to act in all directions and at the same time to shorten the distance to the opponent in order to essentially reach, or better breakthrough, the Main Distance.

Our Chi-Sao, Lat-Sao and Guo-Sao training is geared towards this distance. Training starts in the furthest Main Distance, on the **outer ring of defence**. In application training, we start from the Long Distance so that the practitioners learn to grasp and decide when the Main Distance has been reached and, above all, whether an attack or a defence is required. Who the attacker and defender is can only be designated during an exercise, but not in combat. It is also practised to recognise if a stepping technique has to be used, in case of a delayed attack of the opponent to break through the Main Distance.

The actual fight only starts as soon as the Main Distance is reached or a self-initiated, distance-shortening Stepping Technique is used to attack the opponent.

b. The Short Distance

The Short Distance (also called the 2nd Fighting Distance) can occur after the fight in the Main Distance, or when two bodies meet too quickly. Stress often leads to a misjudgement of the distances. Mistakes, such as making steps too long, can quickly make it impossible to use the front arm regions.

The Short Distance starts at about 30 cm (1') and requires the use of selected Defence and Attack Techniques. Elbows and special leg techniques are used with the aim of ending the fight or regaining the Main Distance, without having to retreating yourself. Elbow techniques are used in WingChun* to control or ward off the opponent's arms or to attack their body directly.

It would be too hazardous to skip the Main Distance by at least 40 cm (16"), because you aim for the Short Distance at the beginning of the fight. However, as mentioned above, Short Distance training is by no means neglected. On the contrary, it is trained with the utmost precision.

In particular, Biu Jee, the 2nd Tactical System (3rd Form) and Mok Yan Jang, the 3rd Tactical System (4th Form) described in the previous chapter, offer a rich assortment of techniques to avoid breaking into the **inner ring of defence** or to allow a controlled transition into the Short Distance. The connection, one could also say the fusion of the Tactical Systems, makes WingChun* and S.A.T complete and with no gaps.

In case a conflict leads us to a ground fighting situation, I developed Combat Training programs a few decades ago to prepare my students for such scenarios. The importance of this training, which includes the most effective close combat techniques, is undisputed. Nevertheless, it never replaces the rudimentary training in the Main Distance in a martial arts class. Rather, martial arts are about avoiding those situations that reduce our technical repertoire and cost valuable time (seconds). At best, the fight ends in the Main Distance.

c. The Long Distance

The Long Distance can only occur before (or after) the fight and is therefore not part of the Fighting Distances. At this distance, you can prepare yourself mentally and physically for the fight, but you cannot (yet) fight unless you reduce this distance, reaching the Main Distance. Due to possible use and calculation of viable Stepping Techniques to shorten the distance, one can imagine a Long Distance of one to three meters (about one to three yards) to the opponent.

However, this distance is not of central importance. Rather, this distance serves to detect an incipient dangerous development in good time. It should be mentioned, however, that the Long Distance is merely a contingency, which is why it cannot generally be expected to clearly identify an imminent escalation as such. Therefore, the focus is obviously on the two Fighting Distances, but also on the timely perception and processing of threatening movements in the Long Distance should be valued and trained.

Shortening a Long Distance to start an attack with a kick is an exceedingly courageous decision, but rarely a wise one. A leg that is used for kicking can no longer be used for moving or standing. Imagine that your opponent begins their attack at the very moment when you are standing on one leg.

The experienced fighter starts a fight with their arms and uses their legs for locomotion, more precisely for attacking with the whole body. The fact that the legs are good tools and can be used for kicking is beyond question. We have countless kicks in the Main and Short Distances. There are no techniques for the Long Distance, which makes it necessary to shorten it. After deciding to attack, we use the legs to shorten the distance (to move the body); and the arms to attack.

There is an exception when defending against multiple opponents. Here, based on the risk assessment, it is possible to choose between three strong kicks of the system; Jing Zang Gerk - Frontal kick, Wang Zang Gerk - Horizontal kick and Che Zang Gerk - Slant kick. These three kicking techniques cover the entire space between our frontal and horizontal kicking angles in order to first create space for oneself and thus tactically deal with the attacks of the opponents, ideally, one after the other.

When training, we implement kicking techniques only at the level of our own hips or, in the Short Distance, at lower positions. This way we use the greatest possible reach of the legs, as quickly as possible. To use the kicks (Jing Zang Gerk, Wang Zang Gerk and Che Zang Gerk), if necessary, we need to extend the Main Distance by 30 cm (1') to about 100 cm (3'3") due to the difference in the length of arms and legs, utilising the propelling execution mechanism. Higher kicks are uneconomical and corresponding to the range of the arms, which precludes the use of high kicks in our system.

Anatomically and according to the laws of gravity, it would be easier to punch your opponent's foot than to kick his head. One reason for this is the division of the fast- and slow-contracting muscle fibres in our body (more on this in Chapter XII). The second reason is the distance from the ground to the opponent's head. Actions of this kind are best suited to other areas, such as the film industry, when spectacular movements and athleticism are required. In self-defence, in true reality, acrobatic movements have no place.

What you should know

In order to place a kick to the head of the opponent, a distance of about 200 cm (6.'7") is covered with the foot, based on an average height (men) of 180 cm (5'11"). A punch, during which one can use the legs as a means of locomotion to shorten the distance, needs less than 25 cm (about 9"). This kick is performed with largely slow contracting muscles of the heavier leg. In contrast, the short and straight path of the fist is performed with largely fast contracting muscles of the lighter arm.

Of course, this explanation is regularly met with the objection of all objections, that someone knows someone who can kick really fast. There is no doubt that there are people who can kick at high speed, and I personally know some of these martial artists, but that does not refute the facts described.

In order to execute a high kick to the opponent's head, one has to manage many disadvantages. The leg has to cover around eight times the distance of a simple straight punch to the same target. The anatomically slower muscles of the heavier leg, which also has to be lifted, while standing on one leg like a stork, even if only for a short time, possess many dangers. An anatomical and physical fact.

Visualization Exercise

Imagine that you see or feel the outer and inner rings of defence and the two spaces in between. As a rough guide, the following always applies; the length of the arms up to the fingers = outer ring of defence, length of the arms up to the elbows = inner ring of defence. Remember the position of Man Sao's wrist, which crosses the dividing line of the two Fighting Distances, guarding it.

Wu Sao is always positioned in the mid-range of the Short Distance (from the body) and Man Sao is always positioned on the dividing line of the Short Distance and the Main Distance. This secures both distances with a corresponding potential of energy. I recognise an advanced student just by how they execute and position their Man Sao and Wu Sao. There is more to these positions than meets the eye. These basic positions are the key to understanding the distances and therefore choosing the correct techniques.

You should learn to look at these two merging distances as a Combat Zone and the two rings of defence as a first and second Protective Shield.

In the beginning, during basic training, you can measure with your arms. But later, when you have got to know your body and are aware of your technical possibilities, you should be able to feel the distances and let them become a part of you.

XI. The Principles of Combat

The principles of combat apply consistently throughout all situations. As a trained martial artist, you can check all your techniques against these principles.

I developed the following eight principles many years ago. The first five of these principles I created about 30 years ago. The last three principles I added at the end of the 90s because of the misguided paths taken by various branches of the scene.

Principles

1. There are two types of attack; the attack to the opponent's body (primary objective) or to their arm position.

2. Defence is the attack against the attacking arms or legs of the opponent.

3. In combat, there is always an attacker and a defender. The person being attacked must first defend the attack.

4. In self-defence, attack without hesitation as soon as the main distance is reached. If you are attacked, you must first attack the attack (defence) and then the opponent's body (attack).

5. Attack from the outside or at an angle if possible, and avoid straight attacks from the centre of your body, as these are too easy to defend.

6. Never maintain contact with your opponent's arms.

7. Always use all your available power to defend and to attack.

8. Never start a defence and an attack at the same time. The defence and the attack each require your full attention. When you are attacked, you must put your energy into the defence, and only when this succeeds can you launch the attack.

XII. Musculature and Function

a. How to use our Muscles

Thanks to our muscles, we can move our bodies. This is made possible by several hundred individual muscles, some of which are controlled voluntarily and some involuntarily. The musculature is the largest organ (if you want to interpret it as such) of the human being, and of all organs, nerves most richly interconnect it.

The fact that human muscles make up about 40% of body weight and that a person has over 650 muscles makes the argument that one has too few muscles to perform a certain sport, seem ridiculous. We find that within other styles of WingChun*, it is claimed that one does not require the use of muscles. This misguidance and contradiction can be easily researched within this field of study.

There are two interesting points of view when looking at musculature and strength. Looking strong and being strong are two very different things. When you are in a gym, take the time to look a little closer at those who are exercising. Many look physically as if they could do an activity like chopping down a tree with a hatchet, but who do you think could actually do this? Have you noticed that strong people don't necessarily look strong? Functional musculature has little to do with the visual size of the muscles. This illusion can be compared to the old phrase 'don’t judge a book by its cover'.

In humans, medical progress is currently leading to truly miraculous possibilities for external changes, whether in the area of building muscles or in the area of body cosmetics. There is certainly nothing wrong with this, but in this age of externals it is not very easy for us to pay attention to our inner body and also to care for and, above all, to understand it.

Our musculature is the organ that burns fat, or in other words, muscles are contractile organs. Without oxygen, essential physiological processes cannot take place. Through exercise, we can ensure that our body has enough oxygen available. We find movement in the majority of sports around the world. What kind of sport is right for whom depends above all on the preferences, but also on the physical condition of the individual. It is crucial to find a sport in which we move, but do not regularly exhaust ourselves because this would result in the exact opposite of oxygen supply and could even damage our health in the long run.

In WingChun* classes, we move in the aerobic zone, which could also be described as moderate to vigorous movement in which we have excess oxygen. Enzymes take care of breaking down the fat. The production of adenosine triphosphate (ATP) then begins, which is the energy source for the muscles. Every physical activity consumes ATP. Glucose is always burned at the beginning of any exertion. If we remain in the aerobic zone during exercise for a longer period of time, the body switches to burning fat to produce ATP and balance the consumption. If, on the other hand, we move for some time in the anaerobic range, i.e. in the oxygen-deficient zone, we will feel tired and weak long afterwards.

This condition is probably sufficiently familiar to all of us. Most of the time we plague our bodies with the motivation to get rid of a few unpleasant pounds and then be surprised that after weeks of training, we felt fatigued, but not really lighter or better. We thought we just had to really torture the body to burn off the unloved fat. However, this is a mistake. The cells needed a lot of time to refuel. Only sugar was burned and as a consequence, we kept the fat. Paradoxically, we mainly lost muscle mass, but the scales did not tell us that. Initially, we were proud of the weight loss, but then it quickly returned. The fat remained, but the muscles that carried it were now missing.

Muscle tissue consumes energy for contraction. This means shortening and developing the force needed to exert traction on the bones, which makes the variety of our movements possible. The muscles keep the body upright and secure the joints. During the many contractions, heat is released, which keeps the body at an optimal body temperature.

Skeletal muscles are characterised by being attached to bones in two or more places by strands of connective tissue called tendons. Simply put, when a muscle contracts, one bone stays in place and the other moves. The attachment site on the bone that is mostly stationary is called the origin, and the one on the bone that is moving is called the insertion. The insertion is usually further away from the body (distal), while the origin is closer to the body (proximal). This is how the body moves when muscles contract across joints (from the insertion towards the origin).
Which movement a muscle enables depends on its position as well as on the other muscles with which it cooperates; the type of joint it crosses is also significant.

Here is a small overview of possible types of movement:

Abduction
The moving of a bone away from the midline of the body.
Example: lifting the arm outwards.

Adduction
Countermovement to abduction. Bringing a bone to the midline.
Example: moving the arm down.

Elevation
The lifting.
Example: lifting the shoulders (as in shrugging).

Depression
Countermovement to elevation. Lowering.
Example: pushing the shoulders down.

Flexion
Lessening of the angle between bones of the arm or leg at the joint.
Example: bending the arm.

Extension
Countermovement to flexion. A straightening movement. Increasing the angle between body parts.
Example: straightening the arm.

Supination
The outward rotation.
Example: turning the hand outwards (arm unbent at the side, the radius moves around the ulna, palm faces to the front).

Pronation
Countermovement to supination. The inward rotation.
Example: turning the hand inwards (arm unbent at the side, radius and ulna cross each other, palm faces backwards).

b. The Contraction of a Muscle

A skeletal muscle consists of muscle fibres lying parallel to each other, which are enclosed in connective tissue as a muscle bundle, and surrounded by the muscle skin (fascia). Vessels and nerves run within the connective tissue and supply the muscles with blood and motor neurons. The length of the individual muscle fibres varies greatly, from one millimetre to several centimetres. In total, humans have millions of individual muscle fibres. The muscle fibre consists of thousands of parallel, rod-like myofibrils that extend along the entire length of the fibre.

Each myofibril is composed of a chain of interconnected units called sarcomeres. Within each sarcomere are parallel rows of contractile protein filaments. These are thin actin filaments (the smallest component of the cytoskeleton, the internal protein skeleton of the cell) attached to both ends of the sarcomere (but not meeting in the middle) and thick myosin filaments in the middle of the sarcomere. Myosin is a motor protein that functions to move material within the cell or cause a muscle contraction.

At rest, actin and myosin filaments partially overlap. When a muscle is stimulated to contract, electrical impulses run to the muscle fibres and cause the actin filaments to slide towards the centre of the sarcomere. This happens because the actin and myosin filaments repeatedly make and break cross connections with each other. This process requires energy and produces a kind of cogwheel effect that pulls the actin filaments towards the centre of the sarcomere. As the actin filaments slide, the myofibrils shorten and contract the muscle. After the stimulation has subsided, the actin filaments slide back and the muscle relaxes.

c. The Interaction of Muscles

Most movements require several muscles to work together in musculature groups. Muscles can pull, but not push. For example, some muscles pull a body part in a certain direction, while others pull in the opposite direction.

Muscles are divided into four groups according to their role:

The Agonist
is the muscle that generates the main force for a specific movement.

The Antagonist
works in the opposite direction. Its mode of action is thus contrary to that of the agonist.

The Synergist
is the co-player. It works together with the agonist. Either it works in a supportive way or it weakens unnecessary movements that can occur during the contraction of the agonist.

The Fixator
is a synergist that fixes a bone to secure the origin of an agonist.

d. Dynamic and Static Muscle Action

Muscles can make use of different working methods. A primary distinction is made between:

Moving - dynamic action
= isotonic muscle contraction

Holding - static action
= Isometric muscle contraction

In practice, it turns out that a purely isotonic muscle contraction only occurs in the rarest of cases. Most of the time, the muscle activity is a mixed form, namely isotonic and isometric contraction.

In WingChun*, our attack can be stopped by a defence and thus come to a brief stagnation. However, we ourselves do not voluntarily stop our attack just because our opponent generates a defence. The visual perception of a defence is by no means an indication that it works. Defence techniques also work in motion, which means that we move until we collide. In both movements (attack or defence), if a collision occurs and the defence is functional, an isotonic contraction changes into an isometric contraction. The muscular contraction, therefore, does not end with the contact of the arm with which we collide, but continues, even if only for a moment. It is the same with an attack that hits the body of the opponent. We do not stop our attack because we have reached the target, but the body of the opponent stops it. Here, too, an isotonic muscle contraction briefly changes into an isometric muscle contraction.

e. Fast and slow contractions

How quickly a muscle can shorten and how long it is able to remain in a contracted state varies from muscle to muscle. This is due to the differences in muscle fibres. One of the differences is the level of myoglobin, a protein that (similar to haemoglobin in blood) contains the oxygen needed for the release of energy.

Haemoglobin is a protein found in red blood cells, whereas myoglobin is a protein found mainly in muscle tissue. About 70 percent of your body's iron is found in the red blood cells of your blood (haemoglobin) and in muscle cells (myoglobin). Haemoglobin is essential for the transfer of oxygen in your blood from the lungs to the tissues. Myoglobin, in muscle cells, accepts, stores, transports, and releases oxygen.

There are primarily two types of muscle fibres:

The red, type I fibres
- contain abundant myoglobin
- Slow-twitch muscle fibres
- fatigue slowly
- are capable of prolonged contraction

The white, type II fibres
- contain less myoglobin
- Fast-twitch muscle fibres
- fatigue quickly
- Are capable of short contraction

Most skeletal muscles consist of a mixture of fibres. For example, in the neck, back and leg muscles (responsible for keeping the body upright) we find predominantly slowly contracting, red fibres. In the arm muscles, which are largely used for sudden acts of strength such as throwing or striking, we find predominantly fast-contracting, white fibres. In the body of healthy people, both groups are in harmonic balance. When overstrained by high-performance sports and especially when there is a lack of movement, deviations in the balance of forces, unilateral movement and overstraining lead to disturbances in the balance. The consequences are malfunctions of the muscular system and the many associated clinical pictures.

Muscular imbalances occur when a muscle in the resting position pulls more in its original direction than, for example, its counterpart (the antagonist). Thus, the strong muscle shortens and the weak muscle overstretches. Within muscle chains in which several muscles (co-players) are responsible for a certain movement, the strong muscles relieve the weak ones, which can lead to the weak ones becoming weaker and thus a muscular imbalance gradually develops as a result.

Unfortunately, this kind of disequilibria often leads to extreme pain, which is brought home to us again and again with the common suffering, back pain. Instead of building up the weaker muscles, the strong muscles are typically stretched excessively or trained with faulty exercises in the same proportion. That this does not lead to a satisfactory result is unmistakable.

With this short excursion into the function of the human musculature, I wanted to point out the essential human movement motor skills. Due to work, poor sleep and unfavourable, sometimes even extreme sports, we are increasingly disturbed in our original sequence of movements.

Movement as a miracle cure

I think that 15-20 minutes of quality exercise every day would be enough to build or maintain our health and quality of life.

Exercise keeps you healthy and makes you happy (through the release of endorphins and serotonin). Exercise ensures healthy blood pressure, cleanses the blood vessels and even creates new ones. The body regains its natural tension, and we feel healthy and strong.

According to the laws of nature, what is not used recedes, including our muscles. If the muscles deteriorate, they are replaced by more or less fat, depending on the body type. This includes the brain, which can also increase fat as well. As soon as the brain becomes fatty, the necessary energy can no longer be generated due to an insufficient oxygen supply. Memory and mental agility are lost. With exercises, we prevent this process and stimulate various metabolic processes.

The paradox of our modern life becomes very clear. In most professions, the mind is required to the greatest possible extent but is not nourished by essential movement. This is followed by sluggishness and usually disturbed eating behaviour (supplying the body with more energy than it needs), which leads to weight problems and thus to additional physical and mental stress. The questions about the meaning of life quickly pile up. We sit at breakfast, at work, during breaks, maybe at the café in the afternoon and on the couch in the evening to "relax". Attending a relaxation class would add to the lack of understanding of the principles of human musculature and health. Relaxation follows tension, which explains the order.

If I were asked for a relaxation exercise, I would first run through simple exercises to first build up isometric tension, starting with the legs, then the lower and upper body and of course the arms. After approximately five minutes, I would stop the exercises and the body would naturally relax. No further explanation would be required.

With the simplest regular physical activities, we could break the cycle of lethargy. Only a select few are in-touch with their own bodies and have the necessary discipline to maintain a routine. Most hand this "task" over to a doctor, who is then supposed to repair the defective part, like a car in the workshop. The intention here is often merely to suppress the unpleasant symptom. The treatment of the cause is not of any importance nowadays. It simply does not interest anyone, neither the doctor nor his patient.

This sensitive topic has preoccupied me for many years. Perhaps because it would be so simple to keep people in refreshing health. Of course, there are diseases that we could not control with this "simple" means, namely exercise. I am only talking about diseases that arise due to a lack of exercise, and there are more than most can imagine. I mention this because I think that martial arts offer a possibility to counteract this muscular and mental degradation. Note that there are many options in terms of healthy physical activities. Martial arts are indeed only one of them. How far the individual would ultimately progress in martial arts is actually inconsequential. First and foremost, it is about movement and keeping one's body healthy. In addition to maintaining health through the ability to defend oneself, martial arts provide another way of maintaining health through movement.

f. Yes, you have enough strength

I cannot tell you how often I have heard the question: "Do I have enough strength?" How does this doubt about oneself arise? What was the cause that resulted in a belief that everyone else is better, stronger, and faster? When you start with a martial art, you are without doubt one of many beginners for a period of time. Everyone starts at the foundation level, none of us is spared learning a skill from scratch and completely attuning it to our musculoskeletal system in order to make it our own.

We are what we do.

If you were to learn this art for about two years, you would already belong to a minority of people who are able to stay with one subject for longer than six months.

In my personal experience, almost 70% of all students resign within a single year of training. In most cases, dissatisfaction arose because things were not moving fast enough. Almost half of those who persevered lost heart in the second year. After years, very few reach or maintain the stage of an advanced student. It should at least be mentioned that those who did not last very long at least started and made an attempt, which I would already like to count as an achievement here. Just little basic knowledge in the field of self-defence can certainly be retrieved for the following one or two years without training.

If you manage to stay motivated and have fun for about two years, you can feel how your motor skills begin to change. You gain abilities that you never had the slightest idea of before. Your self-confidence grows with your skills. You understand the mechanics of your own physique, and you realise that self-defence is primarily about coordination, and controlling your body. The initial question "Do I have enough strength?" has long been forgotten. It is not the size of the muscles but the intramuscular system that is responsible for coordination and the resulting acceleration as well as the function of perfectly flowing movement sequences.

We have arrived in the 21st century and have the intelligence of a modern human being. Do we really want to simply surrender when faced with pumped-up biceps? The question is; what can this muscle do and how useful is "it" in a defence or an attack? Although neither attack nor defence is possible without strength, the size and appearance of a muscle is of no importance. Rather, as martial artists, we are interested in muscular function and precision when performing a technique.

You can only do what you practice regularly. If you learn defence techniques and practice them with discipline and regularity, you will one day master them. When you learn how to move a dumbbell, you'll master that move. It only becomes fatal if you lift weights and then eventually feel capable of defending yourself.

Through regular repetitions, certain movement sequences are programmed into our brains, so to speak. Repetitions of similar movement sequences ensure the emergence of the respective memory programs. No transmissions take place in these reminder programs.

If you want to get better at a particular sport, you can only do so by training in that sport.

Superhuman-looking people are still employed for certain purposes, be it to guard a "door" or even a person. This shows us that to this day the big and strong, as was common in many prehistoric primate tribes, are occasionally recognized as the pack leader. I sincerely hope the advancements that we find in technology, also find their way into the attitude towards reality in the 21st century.

For years, I have been observing how our technical developments are being pushed forward at high speed, while humans on the other hand are becoming slower and less mobile. This is a shame and needs to be corrected.

g. Antagonists, the Opponents

We know that muscles are divided into four groups. Now, in a small example, I would like to deal mainly with the agonists, who are responsible for a specific movement, and the antagonists, the "opponents" (counterpart) of the agonist.

The synergists (working together with the agonist) and fixators (fixing a bone to secure the origin of the agonist) are less considered here, in spite of undisputed equivalence.

Here I would like to make it clear how important it is in martial arts to initially isolate the muscles and then train intramuscular coordination. Progressive training is based on the fact that only the required muscles are used for a specific movement sequence. For the sake of simplicity, I will now explain a punch and also only refer to one agonist involved in the execution, the triceps, and one antagonist, the biceps, even though an ordinary movement like a punch involves many more muscles. Since the biceps as a symbol of masculinity, they are often given the most attention during the weekly trip to the gym. It is therefore a pleasure for me to look at the biceps from a completely different perspective, namely from a functional one.

Let's recall the main types of movements.

The first two were:

- **the flexion** (reduction of the angle)
= bend arm and

- **the extension** (enlargement of the angle)
= straightening the arm.

When you straighten your arm, your triceps contract and your biceps stretch. As you flex your arm (retract your fist), your biceps contract and your triceps stretch.

You don't need good-looking biceps to perform a punch, because it is only stretched during the movement and has no effect on the action itself. However, if the biceps is a visually strong muscle, the question arises whether it can also be stretched accordingly. Because only then our triceps could develop its full potential, and we would be able to punch with a relaxed biceps. A good punch is thus possible with a fast-working (contracting) triceps (in cooperation with some other muscles) and relaxed, uninvolved biceps.

Any slight contraction of the biceps (the triceps "opponent") would result in a reduction in speed and thus weakening of the punch.

With this chapter, I would like to bring you closer to the complexity of our muscles. There's no way I want to keep you from going to the gym. Because training our skeletal muscles is of great importance for our posture and our health. I also cannot and do not want to dismiss the reason for an optical change, which is responsible for our psychological well-being. I regularly train my muscles, and over the past few decades, I have developed my own personal strength training. Improving the technical implementation is the top priority.

With martial arts, the body becomes a harmonious unit. This changes consciousness and the relationship with oneself. The art of fighting helps to create a functional, controllable and economically exemplary skeletal musculature.

h. Coordination

The only way to improve the coordination you need for martial arts is to practice relentlessly, with defined repetition of certain movements.

All you need to learn martial arts is your body, no matter how fit you think you are. Physical performance, strengths, and weaknesses are completely irrelevant. Your functional strength and endurance will increasingly ameliorate with the lessons, which in turn will gradually lead to improved coordination. There is no other way to achieve perfect coordination.

Improving coordination leads to an optimally functioning musculoskeletal system, compensating for imbalances.

In our highly technical world, if none of our required muscles "know" when or how they are actually needed, due to coordination deficiencies, we are not able to use exactly the muscles we need for certain movements. This eventually leads to a physical disaster in a self-defence situation.

In the long run, it's not enough if we just manage to select the right program on the remote control and swipe through the endless content on our smartphones. Today, the main problem lies in the simplification of the way of life. In my opinion, however, the time gained in this way is wasted many times over in pointless, time-consuming activities. So, the questions remain unanswered, "Why the progress and why this time-saving technology in the most diverse areas?" In the end, we are puzzled about what to do with ourselves during this "free" time. The body grows more and more sluggish every year, and the brightest minds will one day invent robots to bring the drink we want to the sofa where we rest our tired and listless bodies.

The fear of the singularity is probably due to the fact that people have been developing diametrically for some time.

Through resistance, we strengthen our muscles, resulting in the movements becoming stronger and easier to perform at the same time. Certain exercises improve endurance, improving and strengthening the cardiovascular system. Exact execution develops functional body mechanics, and muscular imperfections are naturally compensated.

Improving intramuscular coordination is often mistaken for an increase in strength because elaborated coordination allows us to perform certain movements more easily. After tuning the intramuscular coordination, we can actually increase our strength and then go back to intramuscularly coordinating the new tissue (the stronger muscles). An interplay and thus a constant adjustment between the actual increase in strength and intramuscular coordination would be advantageous.

XIII. Strength Training for WingChun* and S.A.T

I have developed special exercises to complement the technical education, with which I can train anyone to become a capable fighter in less than one year.

We call this functional training, Rotational and Synergy Strength Training. This particular training I created together with S.A.T (Special Applications Training Program), a newly developed system that contains the entire repertoire of WingChun*.

What does it actually take for a beginner to develop effective fighting skills in a short space of time? Through the principal findings in my previous chapters, I can make this answer concise.

The training includes one theoretical and two practical parts. In general, all parts are interlinked. The practical parts have little worth without theoretical knowledge, and vice versa.

The parts include:

- Technical training (techniques, combinations, and partner training).
- Internalisation and adjustment of principles and distances.
- Strength training (specific and general).

As a martial arts student, you should listen carefully to your teacher, fully trust, and practice what is taught. As simple as it may sound, it is also quite challenging. Staying focused during class will advance your technical understanding. Together with strength training and interrelated techniques, you will improve the coordination of your complete body. Following the principles and understanding distances, as well as fast and precise execution of techniques, is a constant challenge due to the inevitable and adaptable increase in strength.

You are always challenged and your cooperation and regular, objective review of your technical understanding is the basis for your success. It's a constant cycle in which, like learning a musical instrument, you have your difficulties at first. However, with constant practice, the training becomes easier. Everybody has to take the first step on the path towards becoming a capable fighter, this can be achieved within one year. The ultimate goal is to strive to become a Master. Always be aware that there are other students who are very keen and continue to train for years. If you possess the five virtues of a successful person, which I will discuss at the end of the book, then you will be one of the few who walk the path.

Let's now focus on the execution of an effective punch. In order to perform a hard, strong and technically correct punch, you need the appropriate arm, shoulder, and chest muscles. Of course, there are many more muscles involved in the execution of a punch, but here I will focus on the main ones. The chain of muscles required for a punch starts with the stance, i.e. the leg muscles. From here it goes through the stabilising muscles of the lower and upper body, from the fixators through the synergists to the agonists. An incredible number of muscles serve to stabilise our body, but only a few are used to execute the effective movement. If you accelerate the arm forward in a punching motion, it is only possible with a functional upper arm (here especially the arm extensor), shoulder and chest muscles. The intention when performing the movement is to work powerfully, quickly and precisely. The fist, which ultimately hits the target, is in turn stabilised by the muscles of the forearm.

The focus of this training is therefore less on the isolated use of a specific muscle and more on the training of the cooperation of various muscles.

I recommend that anyone interested in martial arts also obtain a book on human anatomy or, even better, a book on strength training with anatomical explanations. That alone will put a smile on the face of anyone who hears naive statements such as "You don't need strength". Functional musculature is the beginning of everything.

Without strength and tension, you can neither stand nor walk. Without strength and the optimal function of the muscles trained for a certain activity, you can neither put on your shoes nor your jacket in the morning. In self-defence, we undoubtedly use different patterns of movement than in our usual daily activities. I just want to make it clear that for every action, whether it is reaching for a cup, chopping wood or stroking a pet, we employ certain muscles. We demand our musculature and need controlled differentiation. The examples given illustrate how you can move with varying degrees of strengths or gentleness. Every movement has a corresponding meaning. Once we have understood the principle of using the muscles in relation to the action, we can distinguish how and which muscles are used for the corresponding movement, and we are able to control the execution from beginning to end.

The ability to fight requires maximum muscular precision at maximum speed with maximum force.

You do not have to become a bodybuilder to fight. It is not necessary to look physically stronger or be stronger than your opponent. You do, however, need to be strong enough to be a dangerous opponent. You should train and repeat until everything you perform with your body is the fastest, most precise and most powerful version of that movement. Only then are you no longer a victim or a dreamer, but an unpredictable and confident warrior.

In addition to the usual strength training, you do at home or in a gym, I have developed exercises conducive to WingChun* or S.A.T that will make your attack unstoppable and your defence unbreakable.

There are plenty of books on strength training. Most gyms also have excellent trainers to help you build your skeletal muscles.

Now, however, to those exercises which I created in addition to developing stable defences and breakthrough attacks. I mention here, for completion, some more techniques in addition to those already discussed in Chapters VIII and IX. I do not explain their exact function but rather use the movement of these techniques for the development of the forces needed for the above-mentioned objective. Here I start from the familiarity of the execution of the techniques and explain the respective movements for strength-increasing exercise.

To get the most from the strength training, I have added Bong Sao (Winging Arm), a very effective defence technique used against high attacks. Additionally, we complement this strength training with the inner and outer Gwan Kuen (rotating punch) and the inner and outer Tsong Kuen (thrusting punch). These are exceedingly powerful attack techniques with devastating effects.

Some of these techniques have only been mentioned in the previous chapters, but I will now go into their execution.

With Bong Sao, one attacks the opponent's arm from the front, but mainly from below. This is done with the forearm, which, in order to ward off the opponent's attack (defence = attack against the attack), moves rising, swinging in front of one's own elbow. To stabilize the upper arm, it is necessary to place it in front and level with one's own shoulder. Bong Sao comes from the techniques of the double knives of WingChun* (mentioned in the history of the art) and is therefore moved forward, in a rising, cutting motion, like with a knife.

Those who can visualise thrusts, stabs, and cuts (with a knife) in the attack and defence techniques have understood the origin of some techniques of the style. Many movements of the technical repertoire of WingChun* originate from the weapon styles, respectively the forms of:
-Lok Dim Buen Gwan (六點半棍 / Six Point Half Pole) and
-Bat Zam Dou (八斬刀 / Eight Chopping Knives). We recall the history of WingChun* in Chapter III.

To train at home, you simply require only a few items of equipment; a sports mat, two small push-up bars and one or more kettlebells (in the lower weight range). I recommend trying out various weights of kettlebells for these particular exercises. The kettlebells should not be too heavy so that a large number of repetitions can be achieved.

a. S.A.T Rotational Strength Training

- Equipment: Sports mat, kettlebell or dumbbell.
- Techniques: Bong Sao, Tan Sao, Noi Gwan Kuen and Ngoi Gwan Kuen.
- Execution: slow and precise.

Exercise 1: Tan Sao / Bong Sao

Lie on your back on the sports mat. Slightly bend your legs and keep your back straight. Now reach through the bar of the kettlebell with your hand so that you are literally holding the round ball. Note an ordinary dumbbell can also be used and will serve the same purpose. Always train both arms and use the same weight, even if the number of repetitions initially differs.

- Start by moving the kettlebell into the position of a finished punch (arm vertically straight, in the middle of your body).
- Now move the kettlebell back towards your body, forming the starting position (preparation) of Tan Sao.

- Then perform Tan Sao forward and hold this position for a few seconds.
- Then extend your arm out straight into the position of a finished punch.
- Now move the arm back to the starting position of a Bong Sao, elbow in front of your shoulder, turning the hand (little finger side pointing upwards), execute Bong Sao forward and hold this position for a few seconds.
- Then extend the arm once again, turning the elbow into the position of a finished punch
- This exercise for Tan Sao and Bong Sao can now be repeated.
- Change arms after an appropriate number of repetitions.

These exercises can be varied and performed in different ways. For example, repeating Tan Sao and Bong Sao 20 times or more without stopping for a few seconds. In addition, it is possible to train many repetitions without extending the arm as a transition to the next movement. Another variation that will be beneficial to you is the following:

Exercise 2: Tan Sao / Bong Sao

- Move the kettlebell into the position of a finished punch as the starting position (arm vertically straight, in the middle of your body).
- Move the kettlebell back to the starting position of a Tan Sao, change from this position (close to your body)

to the starting position of a Bong Sao, perform Bong Sao and hold this position for a few seconds.

- From the finished position of Bong Sao return to the starting position of a Bong Sao. Change from this position (close to your body) to the starting position of a Tan Sao, perform Tan Sao and hold this position for a few seconds.
- The arm is extended again at the end of the exercise until the position of a finished punch is reached.
- Change arms after an appropriate number of repetitions.

When choosing the weight, you should be sure that you can perform these exercises technically accurate. It would be best to have a small collection of different weights. This way, you could use a lighter kettlebell when doing many repetitions and a kettlebell that is about 2-6 kg (4-12 lbs) heavier when doing fewer repetitions. The point here is not to use the heaviest weight, but simply to perform the rotation exercise precisely. These strength exercises also toughen the very small muscles in the muscle chain (shoulder, upper arm and forearm muscles).

Exercise 3: Gwan Kuen (inner and outer)

Lie on your back on the sports mat, with your knees bent and back kept straight.

I will now provide a short explanation for those who are not familiar with the punch Gwan Kuen (rotating punch, both inner and outer). To perform the outer (Ngoi) Gwan Kuen imagine you have a machete in your hand, and you want to chop a branch, which is about 90 cm (3') in front of you at the height of your head. Prepare the motion with a slightly extended arm, then rotate your arm outwards (Ngoi) away from your body, rising and then forcefully sinking and slashing diagonally across the front of your body onto the branch. Then to perform an inner (Noi) Gwan Kuen you rotate the arm inwards (the blade points upwards during the loop), then rising and forcefully sinking and slashing diagonally across the front of your body, striking down onto the branch. The execution of both movements can be compared to a horizontal (or lying) figure of 8 movement. The entire arm executes this fast and powerful movement through the shoulder and elbow joints.

- Grip the kettlebell and move it to the position of a finished punch as the starting position (arm vertically straight, in the middle of your body).
- From this position, begin the rotational movement (Noi Gwan Kuen) inwards to the opposite side of the arm (the little finger of the fist turns upwards at the beginning of the execution), looping the arm back to the starting position (straight arm). There you stop for one second in the position of the completed strike.
- Now begin the rotational movement (Ngoi Gwan Kuen) outwards to the side of the arm (elbow and little finger of the fist turn inwards at the beginning of the execution), looping the arm back to the starting position. There you stop for a second in the position of the completed strike and start again.
- Noi Gwan Kuen and Ngoi Gwan Kuen (inwards and outwards) can be performed with exaggerated, circular movements.

- Change arms after an appropriate number of repetitions.

Here too there are variations, such as repeating the individual rotating punches, first repeating the inner rotating punch several times, then the outer rotating punch.

b. S.A.T Synergy Strength Training

- Equipment: Sports mat, kettlebell or dumbbell.
- Techniques: Tsong Kuen, Noi Tsong Kuen, Ngoi Tsong Kuen, Go Ping Kuen.
- Execution: slow and precise.

Lie with your back on the sports mat as in the previous exercises.

- Grip the kettlebell and move it to the position of a completed punch as the starting position (arm vertically straight, in the middle of your body).
- Bring the kettlebell down to the Wu position and then immediately after reaching it move forward quickly and in a straight line (Tsong Kuen).
- Now bring the kettlebell back to the position of an inner punch (Noi Tsong Kuen) and move forward quickly and in a straight line (the end position for all punches is always reaching the centre of the body with the arm extended).
- Then bring the kettlebell straight back to the position of an outer punch. When returning the arm in preparation for Ngoi Tsong Kuen, press the elbow inwards

towards the body and immediately after reaching it move forward quickly and in a straight line.

- Then bring the kettlebell straight back to the position of a high parallel punch (Go Ping Kuen) and immediately after reaching it move forward quickly and in a straight line. Make sure that the elbow moving outwards does not touch the floor during the preparation of Go Ping Kuen.
- Change arms after an appropriate number of repetitions.

A variation here would also be to repeat the individual punches several times, such as the straight punch, the inner punch, the outer punch and the high parallel punch 20 times or more. In synergy strength training, a heavier weight can also be used and the number of repetitions reduced accordingly. The order can also be changed at will.

c. Strength Training Without Weights

- Equipment: Sports mat, push-up bar, pull-up bar.
- Techniques: The exercises of the general strength training do not have to correspond to technical movements from WingChun* / S.A.T.
- Execution: Speed can be varied. Exercises can be performed from very slowly to quickly.
- Variations: negative movements such as the fast muscle contraction and the slow to very slow movement backwards.
- Amazing strength gains can be achieved with incremental movements such as doing half the movement,

stopping briefly, doing the movement completely, stopping briefly, moving back and halfway again, stopping briefly and then finishing the movement. Again, it is possible to change the speed of execution.

The best training results are achieved by stimulating the muscle differently from workout to workout. Therefore, one should nourish this concept with one's own experience and knowledge and make every workout an experience.

Training with your own body weight is exhausting but very effective. This training should not be missed in addition to going to the gym. Exercises without training machines or weights often train considerably more muscles than one is primarily aware of when performing the exercises. Especially smaller and shorter synergists, which are frequently excluded with isolating exercises when training with special equipment, are trained here as well. Strength training without weights is excellent for improving comprehensive muscular tension.

In my personal experience, six to eight sets per exercise are sufficient. I cannot give a number of repetitions per set here, but would say, "At best as many as you can manage". Using a sports mat is always advisable when doing floor exercises.

- Crunches with leg raises:

Mainly abdominal oblique muscles and rectus abdominis.

- Push-ups with bars:

Mainly pectoral muscles, arm extensor and anterior muscles of the shoulder.

- Pull-ups (all grip types):

Mainly back muscles, arm flexor, and forearm muscles.

- Lunges and stretch jumps:

Mainly gluteus maximus, leg extensor and calf muscle.

d. Isometric Strength Training

Isometric training has accompanied me on my travels for over 20 years, along with one or two fitness elastic bands. I don't want to leave this type of training unmentioned. A few of these elastic bands fit in any travel bag and allow for a high-quality muscle workout that is also easy on the joints. All muscle groups can be trained with a fitness band, as well strength training without weights and some isometric exercises. If there is not enough time to drive to the gym, and you only have about 20 to 30 minutes to train, the above-mentioned training methods are an ingenious alternative.

In isometric contraction, muscles are tensed but, unlike isotonic contraction (training with own-body weight, weights, and bands) their length is not changed. With this type of training, the muscle is only tensed for a few seconds. I myself work with five to eight repetitions per exercise, with a tension build-up of about six to eight seconds. I don't hold the tension longer than that to avoid over-acidification of the muscle. The reason for this is the reduction in the removal of metabolic waste material during isometric contractions. Over-acidification is averted with timely regulation of the (reduced) blood supply during the exercise and by holding the position for only a few seconds. Isometric exercises are highly recommended and can become part of the expansion of your exercise regime.

Examples of isometric training:

- Stand in a narrow door frame and raise your arms outwards. This exercises mainly the shoulder muscles.
- Standing behind a chair. Grip the top of the chair, arms almost stretched, then press down towards the floor. This exercise is mainly for the back and abdominal muscles.
- Extend the arms forward and press the palms together. The height of the hands can be changed when repeating the exercise. This exercises the chest muscles.
- Take a tennis ball in your hand and squeeze it as hard as you can. Change hands after each set. This exercise builds and strengthens the muscles of the hand and forearm.
- Clasp your hands in front of your solar plexus, one palm facing up and the other down. Now press the lower hand upwards while pressing the upper hand downwards. Then change the position of the arms and do the same exercise. This exercise mainly trains the arm flexor and arm extensor.
- One of my favourites is the following functional exercise for the arm extensor: You position your fist with one arm in front of your body in the Wu Sao position. With the hand of the other arm, you grasp your fist. Now push in the direction of the punch as if you wanted to execute the punch, while at the same time stopping the movement with the other arm. Try to keep the elbows of both arms low during this exercise. Then change position and do the same with the other arm. This exercise is recommended to be practised at three different distances in front of the body (Wu Sao position, Man Sao position and the position between the

inner and outer ring of defence). This exercise mainly trains the arm extensor and the chest muscles.

Once the method is understood, there are no limits to your imagination. If you know how, you can train your entire body in a few minutes and keep it incredibly fit with discipline and continuity. However, I recommend only resorting to this method of training from time to time, keeping the training varied and not practising exclusively at home. In order to train in a concentrated and focused way, a little distance from our private and everyday surroundings is recommended. This is good for the mind and allows new, creative thoughts to arise in us, especially when we are completely with ourselves, as we are during training.

One does not need to do strength training every day. A workout of about 50 minutes, twice a week, would be my minimum recommendation. Let's say you do S.A.T once a week for 90 minutes, go to the gym twice a week for 50 minutes and do my special strength training twice a week for 25 minutes, along with some technical exercises at home. That would be 240 minutes, or four hours of training a week. Not a big effort, but with routine and continuity, you will hardly recognise yourself in two years.

"They must often change, who would be constant in happiness or wisdom."

(Confucius)

XIV. The Mottos

In a real sense, the mottos are the quintessence of much that is described in detail in this book. A detailed explanation of them is therefore not necessary. The mottos serve as a short digest that can be reviewed from time to time to maintain routines.

However, there is one thing I would like to mention at this point: I am aware that for the time being, my opinion and explanations regarding WingChun* do not fully penetrate those who once learnt it differently, heard it differently or even have taught it differently. An opinion that has already been formed is not easy to change, and especially not when what has been acquired for years through constant repetition has been accepted as the undisputed truth.

That is why I would like to state that your opinion is not reflective of your personality. If you change your opinion one day because of clear and irrefutable facts, you do not change your personality. What kind of personality would we have if we only believed in what we first heard, did or in what everyone says and considers the irrevocable truth? Martial arts live through flexibility and the recognition of unexpected circumstances. The skills of a martial artist grow through the acknowledgement and elimination of mistakes and the constant examination of one's own thinking.

A warrior never walks the path in blind obedience.

Mottos

1 If you think you are too weak, you are.

2 Learn to believe in yourself and strive to achieve your ideal.

3 Always improve your technical knowledge and consequently your physical and mental flexibility.

4 Work on the power of your technique, because only technical power is usable power, significant and decisive in combat.

5 Work on your speed without losing power. Technique, power, and speed are the cornerstones of martial arts.

6 Work on toughening your arms through steady and dynamic training.

7 Do not let yourself be influenced by your opponent's movements, and never yield.

8 The exchange between defence and attack, as well as the understanding of the two fighting distances, is the basis of self-defence.

9 To fight, you must have continuous tension. Relaxed muscles are useless in combat.

10 Combat is not harmony. Do not fight if you do not have to. If you have to defend yourself, harmony returns only after the quick and successful end of combat.

11 The purpose of self-defence is to protect yourself, so do not spare the attacker whilst defending.

12 Learn to defend yourself, to protect yourself from attacks that could endanger your health.

XV. Yin and Yang

The Principle of Permanently Complementary Polarity

To all intents and purposes, the forces of Yin and Yang work in opposite ways, and yet they complement each other. They connect continuously and cooperate unceasingly.

These two complementary aspects of each process are in a cyclical relationship, in which the development of one already contains the seed of the other. The body is governed by two systems that determine the flow of energy in an orderly, harmonious manner. Your body consists of individual organs, but at the same time, it is a functioning whole. In a harmonious, flowing balance of the body's own energy, you are healthy and feel well. Health is harmony, evenly flowing energy.

Polarity is the basic prerequisite of all manifest existence. It is the foundation of all creation and the root of all changes. Through it, energy and matter can maintain their infinite play of formation and dissolution, interaction and transformation.

In a harmonious relationship of Yin and Yang, the human being feels healthy and strong. The characteristics listed above are not valences, they are necessities. Without one, the other would be nothing.

Let me briefly explain the meaning of the terms:

Yin Originally: the shady side of a hill	**Yang** Originally: the sunny side of a hill
Moon	Sun
Feminine	Masculine
Dark	Bright
Negative	Positive
Inactive	Active
Water	Fire
Soft	Hard
Defensive	Aggressive
The inner and lower aspects	The outer and the upper aspects

Health is the state of harmonious balance between two poles, the Yin and the Yang. This is expressed in well-being and the alternation between balanced phases of activity and inactivity. Sometimes one will predominate, sometimes the other, and yet neither Yin nor Yang will prevail.

The dynamic Yang energy drives, while the static Yin energy calms. Yang is associated with the colour red. In the case of a Yang overhang, there is an increase in temperature or also inflammation. The tension of the human cell decreases, resulting in a derailment of the entire metabolism. In this phase, one should avoid heat and hectic activity. Instead, one should counteract it with cold, and rest. When eating, one should prefer fruit, vegetables and cold water. If there is a surplus of Yin, there is coldness. Yin is assigned to the colour blue. The human being is sensitive to cold. The cell tension increases. In this phase, one should avoid coldness. One should counteract with warmth, exercise and warm clothing. Cereals and warm water should be included in the intake of food.

Incidentally, the times of day are not insignificant with regard to the relationship between Yin and Yang. At 10 pm, the earth's radiation increases. This means that the Yin increases on the earth and we become tired. By 2 am it increases to double and then drops back to normal by 6 am. When it rains (water/Yin), the earth's radiation increases by about 50 %, and during thunderstorms, it can reach up to 100 %.

It is up to us to find decisive ways to achieve the harmony of Yin and Yang. This applies preventively, as well as in times of stress and also in times of illness. We should often ask ourselves whether Yin or Yang is predominant and try to create a balance. However, we should not forget that harmonisation should be achieved primarily through moderation and not by exaggerating Yin or Yang.

We should learn to listen to our bodies in order to familiarise ourselves with the diverse states within us. The truths of life are the same for all people. Accept things as they are.

It is about getting to know life and thus ourselves.

With increasing age, many people know much better what is good for them and what is not. Be it in nutrition, where nowadays more and more real food is replaced by junk food, or be it in the hopefully not too late realisation that we all need movement to set our organism in vibration so that we can feel, maintain and control it. One of the disruptive factors is the permanent lack of time. Our society has lost its way in many areas due to the speed of information flow and rapid development. Few people take the time to go into themselves, to feel. Owing to this fact, it is easy to understand that fellow human beings and especially their feelings are almost no longer perceived. Decisions are made less from the heart and the feelings, but rather according to statistical circumstances, according to norms and nowadays, especially to ideologies. We can change this at any time if we decide to live in the here and now and accept all its ups and downs.

Negative thoughts trap us and inhibit our true feelings and our development. When ideologies need to be enforced, one can observe how clever manipulation and triggering is used to create fear.

We have to learn to let go of negative thoughts, to let them move on without judging them. The knowledge of perpetual harmony allows us to accept all conceivable situations as they are. Everything balances itself out. Fear inhibits this balance.

In martial arts, you are either male or female, and you are either weaker or stronger, smaller or bigger, younger or older, heavier or lighter than your opponent. There will be a balance. There are at least as many advantages as disadvantages for each aspect. The laws of life always work without condition.

XVI. Dream Factories

a. Recapitulation

In some previous chapters, I have already pointed out errors in knowledge transmission and interpretation.

Most of the defence techniques of WingChun* and especially the most popular ones such as Tan Sao and Bong Sao, as well as some of the attacking variants, originate from the weapon styles Lok Dim Buen Gwan (Six Point Half Pole) and Bat Zam Dou (Eight Chopping Knives). Therefore, many techniques can be compared with stabs (Tan Sao), with cuts (Bong Sao) and with swinging strokes (Noi / Ngoi Gwan Kuen) and are executed accordingly.

With a weapon in hand, no one would wait for contact, then collapse with their arms towards their own body, and then even call that a functional technique. In armed combat, this would be very dangerous and considered as incapacitated or even suicidal.

Fighting without weapons is in no way to be classified as antithetical to fighting with weapons in the application. The decisive difference is often merely buried in whether one holds a weapon in one's hand or not. However, in order to complete a block or an attack, the movements must be made in the appropriate direction. A good weapon fighter does not find it difficult to learn an unarmed art, and a fighter of an unarmed art does not find it difficult to learn a weapon-fighting art. The essential difference lies less in the use of the body but rather in the distance.

In many WingChun* associations, after several years, masters are offered to learn the weapon styles, known as Long Pole and Double Knife, and thus the "secret truth". The fact that this truth is ultimately misunderstood or not implemented at all is what I describe in this chapter. Practising these two weapon styles is as unimportant as learning the other three styles involved in the creation of WingChun*. For me, however, it was, without a doubt, a paradoxical coincidence to have learned the two weapon styles. As is expressed in my organisation, I am extremely conscious of the value of time and not waste it concerning these pseudo-traditional techniques. But in my case, it was more luck than anything else, because that was the only way I could see the dilemma. After learning the weapon styles, I immediately, without wasting time, began to review and inevitably change all the techniques within the system. With the original names of the techniques, it was not difficult to analyse and correct historic misinterpretations.

For many, the myth is a business model, and I can't deny that in this day and age. If you claim it doesn't actually take too much effort to learn, you're probably spreading the word about the martial art on offer a thousand times faster. Just a little pulling and shoving, staying completely relaxed and softly rubbing your training partner's arms, you receive regular certification and feel wonderful, ready to progress onto the next dream level.

One thing that is guaranteed in life - times change. In bad times, people return to what is important and decisive. This change in mindset produces strong people again, meaning the days of the weak and fantasy figures are numbered.

With one stroke, it will be over for the absurd fantasy world of WingChun*.

b. The Cognitive Bias

Many people live according to the motto "What I do not know cannot exist", and this group of people would even claim that some mentioned techniques could not exist because they, the knowledgeable, do not know them.

This is called the Dunning-Kruger effect. The Dunning-Kruger effect refers to the cognitive bias in the self-image of incompetent people to overestimate their own knowledge and ability. This tendency is based on the inability to judge oneself objectively by means of metacognition. The term comes from a publication by the two professors and social psychologists, David Dunning and Justin Kruger - Unskilled and unaware of it. How difficulties in recognising one's own incompetence lead to inflated self-assessments. (Journal of Personality and Social Psychology. Vol. 77, No. 6, 1999, pp. 1121-1134.)

Before I move on to the dream factories, let me say one thing: a big and strong, over 100 kg (220 lb), irritated man who controls his body quite well is a dangerous opponent for anyone. You can pray your "strong equals weak" mantras to yourself for as long as you like. Of course, you can defeat such and similar opponents, that is exactly the reason we learn a martial art. But you cannot defeat such opponents by ignoring factors that require an important regulation of strategy. Some people actually assume that they are better because they have physical disadvantages and therefore simply make use of the attacker's strength. There are many crazy theories and ideologies in this world, and this is one of the most tiresome in our scene.

Since the obvious is undeniably standing in front of me, I name it because it is my duty.

c. The Big Business of Illusion

In fact, I would prefer not to deal with this topic at all, because I know that by pointing out the shortcomings of many styles, I have to expect an outcry from those concerned. On the other hand, I have no choice but to call a spade a spade.

If you feel affected or outraged by the end of this chapter, please consider this as an opportunity to rethink what you are doing and use your emotion to make a change. I was faced with a similar fact one day and had to make a decision. As a mentally strong person, you can allow insight and use it positively.

For about 40 years, various organisations and styles of WingChun* have been establishing themselves. In the meantime, however, there are hardly any training centres in which the true art is taught.

Rather, they have adapted to the inertia and desires of their students and developed styles that are as far from reality as the hawk is from the moon.

This has created a new generation of trainers who are no longer even aware that they don't know anything significant. This is a deteriorating cyclical process because these trainers in turn produce trainers and so on and so forth.

You can manipulate the masses, but not an intelligent minority. That is why I will name here the biggest mistakes of some styles of WingChun*. Already 30 years ago I was fully convinced that this gradually spreading Hokum would disappear into oblivion in only a few years. However, the reason the associations with the most imaginative styles spread at an unbelievably high speed was probably due to the fact that most people are extremely indolent. A quick certificate is more important to them than the hard and sweaty work of acquiring knowledge and skills.

According to a quote from Goethe,
"Everybody wants to be somebody, but nobody wants to grow."

(Johann Wolfgang von Goethe)

As mentioned above, it is ultimately only an intelligent and well-informed minority that cannot be manipulated and quickly recognises the hammock of the illusory world. I myself have had a number of extremely talented students over the past decades. At least 100 of these gifted WingChun* students could easily be masters of my system today, but inertia, impatience, greed or the quest for titles kept them from real success. They gave up or sought the easy way into the dream factories, or one could also say certificate factories. There, they entertain their prey with inane notions about the art of combat.

If you follow a wrong path long enough and others accompany and confirm you on it, the psyche is able to completely block out objectivity one day and create a parallel reality. This is what happened to an incredible number of WingChun* instructors.

The following is a list that you can use to easily identify dream factories. If you are looking for a quick graduation, a quick title or short-cut training to become an instructor or "master" (that's what it says on their paper/certificate), you will be heard in these dream factories. Ultimately, there is little you can do to impress anyone, but who notices and who would ever check? Nowadays, hardly anyone can recognise a real martial art.

I know they exist, those trainers and masters who think like me. You can change everything if you allow it and your insight guides you. This is not to say that we will be infallible, of course not, we are all only human. It means that we are doing our best and learning to improve ourselves all the time.

A sentence from the Roman triumphal processions comes to mind, one of the sentences which were addressed to the commanders in a submissive manner and constant repetition,

"Respice post te! Hominem te esse memento!"
"Look behind you! Remember that you are but a man!"

Let us now turn to what is on offer in the dream factories.

• **They tell you that you can fight without strength.**

In these training centres, people are taught that strength is not good and not necessary at all and that everything is only possible with the "right" technique.

Physical strength is almost frowned upon as "devilish", or "evil".

That is simply nonsense, because the principal pillars of strength, technique, and speed always, and without exception, belong together in a martial art. Without strength, nothing works. Those who have less strength should urgently build it up, even if they can replace the lack of strength to a certain extent with technique. But technique alone is not everything. Some techniques require more speed and others more stabilising strength. Without strength, however, as already mentioned, neither an attack nor a defence will work. In WingChun*, speed means the end product of the transmitted force needed to accelerate a mass (body / but mostly part of a body). The force available at the beginning of the acceleration is decisive for the speed (of the technique) and thus for the result (attack or defence). When buying a car, it is clear to everyone what speed means and by which forces it is generated, but when using one's own body, this is often forgotten or repressed.

Those who do not have or develop enough strength will never become warriors or be able to defend themselves successfully.

In the amygdala, signals are compared with memories. When a threat is detected, a fear-related behaviour will arise. However, this fear is less a thought than a state. Neurotransmitters and stress hormones such as adrenaline and cortisol are released. This leads to a readiness of "fight or flight". Blood pumps through the veins, the heart rate increases, and the muscles are primed and ready. Fighters know this feeling all too well. When you can no longer think clearly and your limbs tremble slightly with tension, you are in a state of readiness to react. Of course, through repetition and exposure to these types of situations, we can learn to manage our physical and mental state. Whether a person decides to flee or fight in a defensive situation is irrelevant. The muscles are ready for whatever we choose. Neither fight nor flight is possible without the use of the muscles.

The belief that you don't need strength to fight or that you have to be relaxed when fighting is hard to beat in terms of ignorance. A psychologist would possibly recognise this attempt to convince oneself that having strength is wrong, is unusable or would even work against oneself, classify this disguise as a "fear of the strong man".

There is a tale that relates to the origin and creation of WingChun* which was simply constructed for advertising purposes. It was claimed that a nun had taught a girl the art of WingChun* and therefore everything was to be totally soft, powerless, and pliable. The names of the women in question were simply taken from the historically relevant Chinese characters (see Chapter III). This was not very clever, as those characters do not offer names, but rather answers regarding history.

Yet even today, I meet WingChun* followers who still believe that their art was developed by a woman after she watched two animals fighting. What more can one say? Most people love stories, the more bizarre and imaginative, the better. I couldn't figure out what they were trying to achieve with this story back then. Maybe they wanted to attract women. What they finally achieved is obvious. Thousands of disciples found themselves attracted to the promise of becoming great heroes, with powerlessness, effortlessness, with trivial movements and locked in reverie. Today, one is tortured by the result of this fallacy as soon as one lands on one of the corresponding social media posts where everyone is allowed to present themselves.

I feel saddened when I witness how everything has come about and what has become of the former art of war.

If you don't believe that strength or mass can be an advantage, you could take a holiday in Alaska and try to run away from a grizzly bear (Ursus arctos horribilis), weight approx. 270 kg (600 lb), speed approx. 56 km/h (35 mph) or even fight with one - and that brings me to the next point.

- **They tell you that you can redirect the power of the opponent.**

The above-mentioned encounter with the grizzly bear should quickly lead to reason again if one survives it. Only those who consume too much television or similar media and have already given up the possibility of questioning things can believe such insane statements. You don't simply redirect power, or your counterpart doesn't have any. But then you wouldn't need the art of self-defence.

The clumsiness of an extremely strong but untrained person who does not know how to use his strength would naturally work against himself in a certain way because he would not be able to use his strength or would not use it properly.

To interpret the disadvantage of a strong, ignorant and untrained person as the general disadvantage of any strong person is exceedingly naive.

In countless situations, the power of an opponent can cause us to move into a new position after our own attack has been blocked by the opponent, or after we have blocked the opponent's attack. So that this power does not disturb our stance or so that we can use the power to bring ourselves into a more favourable position, there are many balancing steps and stances in WingChun*. We ourselves do not redirect any power and do not direct the power of our opponent against himself. We take care of our own power, just as the opponent has to take care of his. It is as simple as that. If you push yourself away from a force in order to maintain your own tension, position and stance, and achieve a new, better position, this is active WingChun*, which could not be more correct. My intention is always my own attack, even if in some situations I use the energy of a movement of the opponent to first secure myself and then again put a technical consideration into action.

So is it now possible to "use the opponent's power" in certain sequences? Yes but only in a certain way and in certain situations, although it is mainly one's own strength and tension that makes it possible at all. Nevertheless, I always answer the question of whether one can use the opponent's power with "No". Someone who generally and exclusively wanted to use this function in a fight could answer this question with "Yes". This, however, would be an intention that I, without knowing the opponent, would have to plan into every fight and thus is not WingChun*.

As an advanced WingChun* fighter, if I had to repel 20 attacks from 20 different opponents, there would possibly be only a single scenario where I could use the power of an opponent's movement together with my own power to put myself in a better position (which I had no intention of doing). In general, the answer to the question "Can I use the enemy's power?" can only be "No". The occurrence of such a situation is already high with 1 in 20 because we are not necessarily the defender, not necessarily slower and not necessarily weaker in the execution of the technique than our opponent is. I point out once again that any technical implementation is not feasible without your own power. If your intention was such, to utilise the opponent's power, there would be no progress, we would simply be treading water and have not valued just how dangerous our attacks are.

What may occasionally occur in combat is not a principle of combat. Contingencies do not belong to the substance of a principle.

- **You are made to believe that there are secret techniques.**

This point is the easiest excuse for the ignorami of this world to conceal their lack of knowledge. Secret techniques only exist where nothingness and ignorance have taken over.

Previously, I was witness to a conversation between two martial artists. The master explained to a young instructor that he should only ever pass on 90% of his knowledge so that he always has a few techniques up his sleeve in case one of his students challenges him one day. That is how he learned it from his master, and that is how he passes it on (so the explanation goes).

During the conversation, it did not occur to either of them that from the 3rd generation of instructors onwards, this martial art can only be a diminished product of the original.

Let's calculate briefly: the master learned only 90% of the art from his master and passes 81% of it on to the younger one, who in turn passes on about 73%. Thus, from the third generation onwards not even three-quarters of the art would be left and a little more than a quarter has already disappeared for all time.

Now this game is far from over, and one day there will be nothing left to philosophise about. All of this is born out of the fear that one would produce a good student who would then want to shame his master out of gratitude. This absurd and at the same time egoistic way of thinking kept me busy for a long time. Interestingly, people also follow those who openly tell them that they are denying them knowledge. And so, in this case, fears destroy a martial art, success and above all progress. Progress would require receiving and passing on knowledge, or even making more of what one has learnt. I will discuss fear, the most destructive thought of all, later on.

A trainer does not know much, and what little they do know could already pass on completely in no time. So, in his misery, he has nothing left but to withhold what he knows and offer worthless information. To the best of my knowledge, students at these training centres are regularly beaten up so that they know who is boss and wait patiently for enlightenment.

It always makes me think of a Latin phrase,
"Quod licet Iovi, non licet bovi."
"What is permissible for Jupiter is not permissible for the cattle."

After all, some stall their gullible students for a long time with the belief in secret techniques. If students were seen as enemies, that would almost be an excellent stratagem. They train for years in the hope that one day they will even learn a technique that works. It's hard to beat the irony of that.

The same applies to those training centres where the eager expectation of advanced techniques is cultivated. Those techniques that you will then be taught one day (so the hope of the devotees) after you have first been held up for a few years with useless movements.

This ruse is similar to the one with the secret techniques mentioned. However, here it is suggested that one first learns the less important techniques in the beginner stage and then the increasingly important ones, the so-called high-level techniques, in the later stages. This depresses the self-confidence of the followers and restricts their growth.

There are more supplementary techniques and programs for advanced students. However, these are merely supplementary, not better. When talking about advanced techniques, one should at least make it clear to the student that these are the complementary techniques for advanced students, but not the better techniques.

Here, you need to understand one thing: The most essential techniques are taught first in any real system, followed by the lesser essential. Of course, it is good if you can add more techniques to what you have already learned in order to understand and connect the system in all its glory.

There are beginners and advanced students in martial arts. The beginners are those who are establishing their understanding of the system, and the advanced are those who have already understood a significant part of the system and are able to link the most important basic techniques with supplementary techniques. The more techniques students can link and apply, the more advanced they are. In the first few weeks and months of training, students learn in a professional training centre, together with the relevant theory, and the Elementary Basic Techniques already discussed in chapter VIII.

Subsequently, some additional, supplementary techniques, make up almost a third of the total technical repertoire of the system. The first year is primarily about internalising the basic techniques with specific exercises. Following this indispensable foundational training, new techniques are taught, which in turn, underpinned by optional combinations, progress a beginner into the advanced stages. The student gradually becomes an advanced practitioner, the technique is and remains just the technique and only comes to life with the skills of the user.

An advanced student is characterised by their understanding and flawless application of the elementary basic techniques. The teaching programme is clearly defined, but it is still up to the student to improve their skills until the level of an advanced student is reached.

- **They keep you busy pushing and pulling.**

Unfortunately, I have to mention the "pushers and pullers", even though I really dislike dealing with this topic. I do not want to completely exclude the possibility of pushing and pulling in a fight, but we should by no means consider it necessary to focus our precious time on mainly pushing and pulling exercises. With little action from the defender, they usually push over the arms. The defender does not punch or kick at the person pushing (as should be the case) but retorts with a pushback or even tries to cushion or yield this with their arms. Unfortunately, I have to mention this version of employing gullible students, is now seriously practised in many organisations. I myself could not believe it when I was first told about it.

And of course, they start with contact to practise these meaningless exercises by touching each other's arms. The contact of the arms just happens because they like it that way. To start with an attack or a defence is no longer practised among these followers.

From what I have explained about combat, it may sound funny or absurd to you as an attentive reader, but they simply skip attack and defence and just start touching each other's arms; and this has become common practice in pretty much all WingChun styles.*

Imagine a battle, in ancient Japan (in the Sengoku Period, known as the Warring States Period) about 500 years ago (1467-1603), with the following sequence of events: The soldiers of two rival warlords charge at full speed to each other, shouting then skid to a stop and begin to start pushing and pulling. Cutting, stabbing, punching, defending and kicking are non-existent - No, only pushing and pulling is done. It obviously doesn't make sense and would only be seen in a comedy sketch, right? In those days, you certainly wouldn't have impressed anyone with these trivial exercises. At best, one would have been decapitated for trying to waste the soldiers' time with these games. Everyone can answer for themselves why it is possible nowadays to occupy martial arts enthusiasts with such ludicrous movements.

They want to first push and pull and then maybe eventually attack properly. Even if some would like to avoid raw combat, such exercises completely miss the point. It is occasionally possible to train how to react to pushing and pulling in a confined space, but only rarely. Regardless of whether you are awarded the best pusher in your small group, it is not relevant in a real confrontation. Primarily, it is imperative to attack and defend fiercely.

Nobody in their right mind starts a martial art because they want to learn how to push and pull. These are and remain fractional aspects of fighting.

• **You are told you have to be passive.**

It is difficult to say which of the points mentioned so far is the most audacious with which to entertain trusting students.

In these training centres, they want you to believe that you can passively react as soon as an attack accidentally hits one of your positions. I write "accidentally" here on purpose, because the positions are often motionless or, moreover, placed much too low in front of the body. The collapsing of the arms (upon contact with the attacker's arms) is what followers of this faction call yielding, a "passive defence". No real fighter could be talked into such unrealistic nonsense. Only those would-be martial artists who do not possess the basic prerequisites and are extremely reluctant to exert themselves can be turned into devout followers with the aforementioned games and shifts in reality.

If you try to stop an attack as soon as it accidentally hits one of your positioned arms, then you won't be able to defend yourself.

Whatever they call it, passivity, yielding or otherwise, it categorically doesn't work. Anyone who believes in it was just lucky that they never really tried it or didn't have an opponent to be taken seriously. Of course, it works within a group of like-believers and of course, the believers always attack their instructors and masters in a certain way, so that it appears to work wonderfully, underpinning their own faith. But in the harsh reality outside the sacred spaces, it does not work.

At this point, I cannot pass up the opportunity to explain a process that is often classified as passive in these dream factories which, on closer inspection, is the exact opposite.

In WingChun there is a stance and a turn, which leads to another stance. Technically, this combination goes from Jing San Ma - the basic stance, to Juen Ma - the turn, to Zak San Ma - the side stance. Now, we assume that your Tan Sao does not completely slow down the strong attack of the opponent. No big deal, because that just leads to the predominant force flowing into the shoulder of the defending arm, which in turn directs that force across the entire upper and lower body under tension, the pelvis and farther to the legs. This then leads us to push off from that, and turn from Jing San Ma through Juen Ma to Zak San Ma. We have now turned and are no longer standing at the same angle (arm and body) in front of our opponent, and the coinciding force (ours and the opponents) can no longer affect us. Rather it has helped us to take up a better position for this scenario. My perfect Tan Sao leads me into a side stance. You are your Tan Sao, you are your turn and you are your stance. It didn't just happen; you practised it, you did it within a split-second and afterwards, you are standing stable (under tension) in a new stance which offers you good preconditions to move again.*

Erroneously, the passivity lovers assume that all this was done by the opponent, the one who actually just wanted to punch them in the face. Well, without my opponent, it wouldn't have happened, but who did what? If I were standing in front of a tree to practise Tan Sao with Juen Ma to reach Zak San Ma (Tan Sao with Revolving Stance from the Basic Stance to the Side Stance), I would slightly undercut the outer ring of defence similar to a collision of defence and attack. Then I would push myself away from the tree with my arm (Tan Sao) in a technically precise manner in order to link all involved techniques. Did the tree help me achieve my Side Stance? Did it do anything at all? Did it move me? The only thing the tree did was to offer me resistance and stability. What I did was actively perform a technical combination using my body tension and my strength. There is nothing passive about this simple yet perfect combination that puts you in an excellent position to launch a counter-attack.

I would recognise passive behaviour when someone punches someone else in the face and the passive recipient then hits the ground without resistance. It doesn't get more passive than that.

If you have the opportunity to observe how those who have raved about passivity for years behave as soon as they learn the wooden dummy form (Mok Yan Jang) and are finally allowed to be active, you will be very surprised. Suddenly, there is no trace of passivity and the redirection of the opponent's power that one wanted to inculcate in one's students. Even with Tan Sao, the wooden dummy is actively attacked without question.

No sooner has someone learned the 4th Form (Mok Yan Jang) than the wooden man is beaten as if there were no tomorrow and all of a sudden, they even do all the defence techniques in the right direction.

What is astonishing is that even at this stage, awakening is usually absent, and the brainwashing continues to work even when one is actively doing the opposite of what one thinks to believe in - what irony.

The Danish philosopher Kierkegaard once wrote, "There are two ways to be fooled. One is to believe what isn't true; the other is to refuse to believe what is true."

(Søren Kierkegaard)

Résumé

An attack must be stopped with movement, strength, and technique. In the real world, this is called a defence technique.

Of course, in principle, everyone can do what they want. The only thing that troubles me is that people drag others, and thus also gullible, principally interested and unfortunately also talented martial arts students, into their private fantasy world. Some people have created a martial arts cult that is meanwhile widespread but insubstantial by exploiting the ignorance of others for profit.

It is hard to find qualified instructors in the martial arts world who were taught by true traditionalists or sought the right path on their own. Although I believe, I can occasionally detect a slight hint of change.

"*You must be the change you wish to see in the world.*"

(Mahatma Gandhi)

All those who found a way out of the clutches of these dream factories through their own strength and conviction deserve my appreciation. I know that these enthusiasts exist, even if we do not know each other personally.

I am absolutely certain that some have already been following better paths than the largely prescribed ones for a long time. When in combat, it's important to keep in mind where most hits find their target, the distance, and conditions under which danger is imminent, and the height at which your arms protect you. Then check and build everything logically from the beginning.

It is so easy to see that "the Emperor is naked". But for that, we have to step out of the obedient crowd and dare to mention it.

VIVERE MILITARE EST

XVII. From WingChun to S.A.T

The training centres of the International Academy of WingChun have been offering S.A.T exclusively for quite some time. Since the 90s, I have been trying to maintain the art in an indignant struggle and to make it clear that my instructors and I offer something completely different from what interested people know from many training centres. But that was literally like trying to flog a dead horse. After a quarter of a century, I will end this endeavour to set things right with one laughing eye and one weeping eye. I am simply tired of it. I no longer oppose the demise of WingChun*, but watch the spectacle from afar.

In my description of the dream factories, you can see what I think of the remnants of a lost era. It is crucial to believe in oneself and the principles one holds. However, progressive, inductive and objective thinking is needed. One must keep one's feet on the ground and not forget who and what one is. Using visualisation exercises to see the fruits of what you are planting even before germination is of great value. Under no circumstances, however, should daydreaming be confused with visualisation.

"*Primus error veniam meretur.*"

"*The first mistake deserves forgiveness.*"

Of course, one can or rather must make mistakes. But mistakes must also be recognised as such. If a condition does not show any positive change despite countless repetitions of the given actions or ways of thinking, it is clear that a mistake has been made and needs to be corrected. To continue to practise a martial art that has been exposed as principally incorrect, just because one has invested time and money in it and possibly reached a high degree, is simply unwise. However, this is what I have been witness to for a quarter of a century now. From now on, I will no longer try to convince others during my countless trips to the most diverse countries. Instead, I will inform the interested parties and observe how the game continues and what excesses are still to be expected. The outcome remains uncertain; it depends on the openness and readiness of you. I remain optimistic.

The S.A.T (Special Applications Training Program).

S.A.T refers to the ultimate applications of my complete WingChun system, as well as my Close Combat and Weapon Fighting Programmes developed during the 90s. It encompasses, so to speak, the unlimited totality of what we have to offer with the International Academy of WingChun.

S.A.T is the essence of what I have developed and taught for decades.

Adapted to modern times, S.A.T is a martial art that trains applications from all areas of self-defence from the very beginning. Even though unarmed skills and the basic techniques of WingChun make up the largest part of the training, it is necessary to train in the safe handling of sticks and other weapons (i.e. knife) at the beginning of the curriculum. Only in this way is it possible to practise defence against striking attacks within the first few training sessions, especially understanding the purpose and operational distance of each weapon. The skills in handling these tools train depth perception, coordination, and reaction in a very short time.

With my military background as a lone fighter and as a teacher at the German Army School, in combination with my more than 50 years of experience in martial arts, I have asked myself how I could train special units, personnel of exclusive security companies, or generally interested people in self-defence. My goal is to prepare them as quickly and optimally as possible for their respective requirements. I believe that my work as a Grandmaster and founder of the hard and uncompromising systems of WingChun, combat and weapon fighting, can be useful in this regard. I have come to the conclusion that, due to time constraints, it is not necessary to train the complete WingChun system or, for instance, the weapon fighting system (Escrima) with all its traditional facets.

Since no graduation system is required for S.A.T, I was able to exclude graduation-relevant elements and at the same time renew my teaching concept in order to drastically shorten the training time. This has resulted in a new art with which I can equip everyone with special skills in a very short time, completely independent of previous knowledge. Ultimately, S.A.T also serves as training for practitioners of other martial artists, helping to free themselves from their potential limitations of sportive martial arts. However, the structure of S.A.T also enables inexperienced people to enter the realm of self-defence.

With S.A.T I officially released a new era of self-defence training at the highest level to the general public in 2014.

There are no classical graduation examinations in S.A.T. Nevertheless, there are various markings in the form of a badge for instructors and leaders of training centres. There are also badges for students that indicate the level of training after basic, advanced and finally combat training (Primary, Upper, and Combat Level) has been completed.

We train effective applications with specially developed programs. Our students learn the principles, the elementary basic techniques, as well as the complimentary techniques of combat to be optimally prepared for a wide variety of self-defence situations.

With S.A.T I have made it my life's mission to preserve the true art of fighting and the entire technical repertoire of WingChun* in all of its martial perfection.

"*One change always leaves the way open for the establishment of others.*"

(Niccolò Machiavelli)

XVIII. The Power of Thinking

If you think you are too weak, you are

This sentence is the first of my 12 mottos, which have been instilled in each of my training centres together with the eight principles since the International Academy of WingChun was founded. Our instructors always have the task to ensure a clear positioning and at the same time a characteristic differentiation from other existing arts using the structure of the system, the mottos, and the principles.

Human beings are because they think.

When one thinks something, there is always a reason for it. Either one is already a member of the "supervised thinking" program through constant use of TV and Social Media or one is able to interpret circumstances oneself, i.e. to think for oneself. With the ability to think for yourself, you would be lucky, along with others, I estimate less than 10% of people, who are little or not at all manipulable.

There is an essential difference between being convinced and being manipulated. Allowing oneself to be convinced requires that one thinks and decides for oneself. Only those who are in spiritual growth can allow new thought patterns, even if they were previously of a different opinion. Allowing oneself to be manipulated presupposes that one thinks reluctantly and cannot make one's own decisions. Those who have reached spiritual stagnation cannot allow other thought patterns than the ones given.

Thinking for oneself and analysing oneself causes conflicts, which the manipulated person knows how to avoid cleverly. Conflict can cause hard physical or mental work (consequences) and this is what most people try to avert. One would be forced to leave the comfort zone and prepare for any changes. A positive change can mean many things. It could initially mean the loss of so-called friends who no longer understand you (which would often already be the first step to success). Or it could be a new beginning (e.g. moving house, changing job, a new partnership, etc.), which most avoid by just getting on with it, going through with it or sitting it out, so to speak. Despondent people dream of retirement, winning the lottery and other evidence that what they are doing is not fulfilling. Those who love what they do would never look forward to retirement, that is, the end of the activity they love, and winning the lottery is merely an attempt to obtain without effort what one misses deep inside. Both desires are typical of the manipulated and inert masses.

Your life is neither your retirement nor your lottery win. Don't wait for a day in the distant future that is supposed to change or improve your life. Have you ever asked yourself what should be different when that day arrives (e.g. when you retire)? Waiting for "salvation" will not let you grow and certainly not bloom. You can progress if you learn to give your life a clear structure and goals, or at least partial goals. You can immediately change and improve your life by becoming aware of your creative mental capacity.

Practice visualisation and try to see more and more clearly what you want and who you want to be. This can be difficult at first, and it is at the beginning of this process a fighter's heart will be needed. In your visualisation exercises, imagine that you must first free yourself deeply from the wreckage of your own false thinking. Once you have freed yourself from this, your progressive and positive thinking will lead you exactly where you want to be. Persevere and do not give up even when the sky seems to be falling on you. When your will is clear, doubts will fade and doors will gradually open.

Sure, there's a wealth of books available about positive thinking now. What I can advise you to do is to take your thoughts seriously. Our rational self has to learn to communicate with the subconscious, to tell it where to go. Thinking is a coherent, active and controllable process. Correct or better inductive thinking is one thing, but another essential point to clear the disturbing stones of one's own thinking is to consciously avoid destructive, negative thoughts. Stop them immediately when they begin to arise.

Here is a small example from a treatise that a student from San Francisco gave me about 25 years ago to read on the flight home: The treatise was about the ageless body and mainly about the fact that we set the ageing process in motion or accelerate it with our prejudicial thoughts. How often do we hear: "I'm already xx years old", "At my age, it's no wonder that ...", "You should get to my age first", "When I was young I could ...", "At your age you can't ...", "It's getting harder and harder...", "At our age, we should take it easy" etc.? These are the very thoughts that age us at a rapid pace and also make us ill.

I myself know people who have one of these sayings ready every day, and what can I say, that is exactly how they exist. Our main problem is the possession of an identity card, the knowledge of our age and of older and particularly ailing examples of our species. People today do little or hardly any exercise, but are surprised to find that one day they can no longer perform some activities as well or at all, despite not performing them for several years. This in turn encourages people, who have a relatively good level of education, to think destructively that age is to blame. They are stuck in reverse and don't realise it.

You don't need an identity card. Your habits are your identity.

The time when one was still healthy, strong, sporty, good-looking and always on the move is just filed away as the past and done with. It simply cannot be any more. Nevertheless, people like to talk about the past and explain how great they once were.

I have never forgotten the thesis, nor have I ever allowed destructive thoughts of this kind. This was, of course, only a small passage of a wonderful article on the consequences of destructive thinking. We feed our subconscious with negative thoughts just as we do with positive thoughts. Those who cultivate positive thoughts, but also allow destructive thoughts to arise, take one step forward and two steps back. Positive thinking makes no sense if you do not first learn to control negative thoughts. Eliminate negative thoughts and nurture, create and allow positive thoughts. This is not an ordinary task, because in reality, it is hard work and you have to practise day after day. It is not easy precisely because we constantly have to recognise and deal with the most diverse attempts at manipulation.

Fear is the most destructive of thoughts.

For example, one morning you hear a news announcement on the TV:

"Breaking news! Dear residents of town B, the tank of a plane filled with a special fertiliser has ruptured. The plane departed from airport C and flew over our town in order to reach a field in neighbouring town A. Please stay in your homes or workplaces and close the windows for the next two hours. However, if you feel a scratchy throat or even a slight itch in your eyes during the day, please see your doctor."

If it later turns out that the broadcast was just disinformation or a misunderstanding, how many people do you think would have nonetheless experienced some of these symptoms and gone to the doctor? Most would insist that they felt those exact symptoms. This is the power of manipulation and ultimately of thought. Our thinking can create symptoms of illness and unhappiness, but also healing, happiness and success. It is all about right thinking.

You can learn to observe and control your own mind. You can control thoughts, stop bad ones, nurture good ones and rationally steer towards success.

In fact, it's all about what you think about yourself. What others think about you is completely irrelevant.

Successful, whatever the word may mean to you personally, will be achieved if you think right and as a result, act right.

Doing nothing leads straight to nothing.

For the majority, with proper thinking and the creation of a clearly visualised goal, it would take just a few weeks to positively change or enhance their lives.

Your faculty of thought and your creative power are limitless.

We think because we are, and we are what we think. Everything we are arises in our thoughts.

"*Magic is believing in yourself. If you can do that, you can make anything happen.*"

(Johann Wolfgang von Goethe)

XIX. The Way of the Warrior

a. The Five Virtues of a Warrior

Will

Courage

Diligence

Perseverance

Honour

The five virtues are self-explanatory and are the companions that point you in the right direction so that you can recognise what you really want. They help you to:

- Identify and go your way.
- Enforce and do what matters.
- Go for it, even if you feel alone at first.
- Never lose sight of the ideal, even if the path is rocky.
- Always remain trusting, loving, humble and grateful.

b. The Way of the Warrior

Go through life with your head held high and adopt the attitude of a self-confident person in everything you do.

Regularly check the path you are following is really yours and conforms to your personal ideal. If it is not, and you begin to stray, correct it without wasting time.

Never let the opinions of others throw you off your path. The more success you have on your own path and the more self-confident you are, the more people will try to dissuade you from your path, luring you onto theirs or putting obstacles in your way.

Look carefully at people who want to give you advice. Outward appearance, e.g. the type of clothing, can also be a clever disguise, but essentially reflects a person's self-confidence and social competence. So, check how they dress, check how they look after themselves, check their attitude and behaviour, and then decide whether to listen to them.

Do not trust people who live in causeless fear. Rather, stay away from people who are afraid of diseases that might infest them. Avoid those who are afraid of change, afraid of other people, or even afraid of their own lives. The greatest evils of humanity arise from fear. People without courage and people manipulated by fear hold you back and rob you of your energy. People without courage never follow a warrior, but only feed on their strength and energy as long as it is available.

Follow those who are already leading by example on your chosen path, or those who have already mastered what you wish to learn.

Develop routines for all areas of your life where you want to grow and maintain your discipline.

Realise that insight is the origin of unfoldment.

Consider any problems you face as training for your mental flexibility.

Avoid hating anything or anyone, and immediately replace negative thoughts and thoughts of doubt with positive and creating thoughts.

Trust your instincts.

The path must be walked,
otherwise it would not be the path.

I end my book with a quote from Niccolò Machiavelli,

"*But since my intention is to write something useful for anyone who understands it, it seemed more suitable for me to search after the effectual truth of the matter rather than its imagined one.*"

(Niccolò Machiavelli)

I would be extremely pleased if I have awakened your interest and inspired you to change your way of thinking or even to embark on a new path.

It was an honour to share my thoughts with you.

Sifu K. Brand

冠佈郎詠春師傅

References used

Dunning, D./Kruger, J. (1999): *Unskilled and unaware of it. How difficulties in recognizing one's own incompetence lead to inflated self-assessments. Journal of Personality and Social Psychology, 77* (6), 1121–1134.

Kornhuber, Hans H./Deecke, Lüder (1965): Changes in the Brain Potential in Voluntary Movements and Passive Movements in Man: Readiness Potential and Reafferent Potentials. *Pflügers Archiv, 284*, 1–17.

INTERNATIONAL ACADEMY OF WINGCHUN®

S.A.T

YOUR OWN SECURITY

SPECIAL APPLICATIONS TRAINING PROGRAM

Sifu K. Brand

sifukbrand@wingchun.international

www.your-own-security.com

Printed in Great Britain
by Amazon

a6c16e28-a123-4707-8ce6-3c04006d1f1aR02